T0283009

INTERNATIONAL BEST-SELLING AUTHOR

SONYA D. WRIGHT

IT'S NOT OVER UNTIL
GOD SAYS IT'S OVER

God Always Has The Final Say

Copyright © 2024 Sonya D. Wright

All rights reserved.

Sonya Wright maintains all moral authority over the contents of this book.

No part of this publication may be reproduced or transmitted in any form or by any means electronic or mechanical, including photocopy, recording, or any information storage and retrieval system now known or invented, without permission in writing from the publisher, except by a reviewer who wishes to quote brief passages in connection with a review written for inclusion in a magazine, newspaper, or broadcast.

Print ISBN: 979-8-35095-287-2
eBook ISBN: 979-8-35095-288-9

Printed in the United States of America

*"For I know the plans I have for you," declares the Lord,
"plans to prosper you and not to harm you, plans to give you hope
and a future."— Jeremiah 29:11*

DEDICATION

This book is dedicated to my mother who spoke life into my soul by telling me to always trust God.

To my beautiful daughters Rudy and Faith, who are the miracles the Lord gave me and have blessed my life more than I could have ever asked for.

To my greatest supporter and God's gift to me, Lee Andre Wright, who motivates me to be the best version of myself, loves me unconditionally, and treats me like the queen God made me to be, I am one blessed and highly favored woman to be your wife.

TABLE OF CONTENTS

ACKNOWLEDGEMENTS

First and foremost, I would like to thank my Lord and Savior Jesus Christ for being the lover of my soul. I give Him thanks for making me fearfully and wonderfully (Psalm 139:14), and for all that He has done to shape and mold me into the woman of God He created me to be. The Lord gave me the courage to confront my fears head-on and the perseverance to overcome them. I am appreciative of the life the Lord has blessed me with and the opportunities He has provided for me to grow and learn from every experience. In the same way God has loved and forgiven me, I am able to love and forgive others through the power of His Holy Spirit. I am so grateful to be chosen by God as His vessel to declare His goodness and saving grace.

I want to express my gratitude to Chelsea Fleeman. You are a beautiful soul and a blessing in the lives of those you encounter. I will be forever grateful for our sisterhood. Thank you for believing in the vision that the Lord has given me and for supporting my book. Your talent for art is truly a gift from God.

Thank you to my mom and beautiful daughters for walking alongside me and always being my safe place. Your love and support for me throughout the most difficult periods in my life means more to me than you could ever realize.

Thank you to my mother-in-love, who welcomed me to the family like I was her own daughter and for raising an amazing man that I call my husband.

My gratitude is endless to everyone who has prayed for me, shown me love, supported me, and believed in the vision the Lord has given me to share with the world.

Lastly, I would like to thank my better half, my gift from God, my husband Lee Andre Wright for his unconditional love for me. I am so grateful for you, Babe. You bring out the best in me and I am so thankful that I get to do life and ministry with you. I love you!

By Derrine Wood

It's not over till God says it's over.

What can I say about Mrs. Sonya Wright! First, she's a woman of God. Jesus has all of her. From the most vivacious smile to her engulfing laugh, you are always in the presence of joy!

My first encounter with Sonya was an immediate heart connection. Two sisters whose love for Jesus connected. I knew immediately that there was love, truth, and grace in her and she never made me or anyone else feel like she was all that and a bag of chips! Her compassion for seeing people right where they're at is amazing. She's been through it! But those scars are used to uplift the mighty name of Jesus. Because, in her, it's all about God. Nothing about her. She has surrendered it all and obedience is the strength of who she is! She's a prayer warrior, too! Either in her private time or in public, the names of her family, her friends, her children, and her enemies are lifted to the throne of the king because she values prayer with the father.

I am blessed to have her friendship and her love. I can't imagine life without her. We might not talk forever, but when we do, it's just like we never skipped a beat from the last time we spoke or saw one another. God has knit us together. Count it all joy when God brings you someone like Sonya! You too will give shouts of praise and adoration for all that happens!

It's not over until God says it's over!

By Sandra Pawar

There are far few books out there that make you feel like within the pages you have found a friend, a mentor, a sister, but when you do find that one, you hold on to it for dear life. This is what I know the pages of this book will feel like, that it will be just like sitting down with a dear friend, a true sister, and just catching up and listening to their story, but it will also be so much more.

Within these pages you will hear of God's faithfulness, His goodness, His grace, His victory, and His deep love for you. You will hear also of brokenness and tears and heartache, but you will see proof of God's redeeming love and the way He restores and lovingly puts back the broken pieces of one's life.

I am a fortunate person because I have not only read but I have seen firsthand what God has done in Sonya's life, and it has been truly amazing. I have also seen what Sonya has done with the life God has given her and that, too, has been remarkable in every way.

Sonya Wright is a powerful and anointed woman of God. She speaks and you hear Jesus; she acts, and you see Jesus at work. Not only is she my friend, but she is also my mentor and my pastor, and I am so glad that I get to share her with the world through these pages.

Sonya will lead you to a deeper life in Christ through these pages and she will have you shouting His praises and singing of His glorious wonder.

You will meet Sonya within these pages, but more importantly, you will meet with Jesus.

As you read this book, I know her prayer for you would be that you would allow the Holy Spirit to meet you right where you are and that you would allow him to reveal to you the beauty and majesty of Christ, and that it would forever change your life, like it did hers.

So, now, turn the page and breathe . . . and find Jesus who loves you.

FOREWORD

By Bishop James Black

When asked to write this foreword, I reflected a lot, primarily to determine my ability to adequately and sufficiently produce collective thoughts and praises that would pique the curiosity and interests of those who do not know the writer well enough to go beyond the foreword, to boldly discover: "Why it isn't over until GOD says it's over." To also explore the writer's audacities and purposes to think that a reader would want to and need to know why there is still some hope and potential for victory after all the reader has been through.

Sonya lays out masterfully and relatable her ultimately victorious journeys, through her difficult valleys and apparent hopelessness of both spiritual and personally painful Job-like trials and myriad tribulations. Having witnessed much of the latter journey to the near mountain top treks; both personally and spiritually, I take pleasure and joy in writing this foreword. Her faith, unwavering integrity, and ability to love her worst enemies and emerge victorious with a wonderful Godly husband and a co-pastorate, is beyond one of GOD'S great modern-day Job-like MASTERPIECES. You will see why co-pastor Sonya could emerge from her latest cruise with her new loving husband, after so many years of hoping and tears, to write this loving, heart-wrenching MUST-READ: It's Not Over Until God Says It's Over. Enjoy!

By Faith D. Edens

Along with giving birth, a mother also makes a lifetime commitment to raise her child. A mother's love is the only unconditional love in the universe. My mother is my role model, my best friend, my inspiration, and my guiding light through the dark. Everyone has a superhero in their life and as you read this amazing biography you, too, will see why my mother is my superhero.

FOREWORD
By Rudy King

Sonya Wright is my mother, and she is an amazing storyteller, who brings truth and light to the pages God has given her. This book is worth reading, especially if your walk in the Lord continues to attract growth. Within the chapters you will relate, cry, ask questions, and understand what it's like to be a daughter or son in the Lord. While reading this book, I pray that you're open to what God wants to reveal even in your life.

By Lee A. Wright

There may be several reasons you are reading this book right now. Maybe you just "happened" to come across it as you were scrolling through your feed or walking through the bookstore aisle? Perhaps you know the author and you are already familiar with her work and journey? Could it be the title or picture that caught your eye . . . "It's Not Over Until God Says It's Over?" Or maybe, just maybe, you were inexplicably drawn to it by a power greater than you, that whispered in a still small voice and told you that the answer to what you have been seeking can be found in these pages? Whatever your reasons are, it is sure to bless you.

I am so very grateful to my wife for asking me to write a foreword on this project. I'm reminded of the words spoken by singer, songwriter and pastor, John P. Kee, some years ago when he said; "In this life, everyone shall have a valley experience. I want you to know that while you're going through it, Jesus has said, "I will never leave you nor forsake you." So powerful and true for all of us. None of us are exempt! To that end, I will let you in on something I shared with Sonya about one month after we met. We'd both been through our own share of heartache, pain, and disappointment. I told her, "I can see that you are trying. I don't take that for granted. I know that you've been through a lot and to trust again is not always easy. I can respect that and accept that. You've been hurt! I pray that I'm never the cause of that hurt ever happening again. You can call yourself a Queen because you ARE a Queen! "Celebrate Your Crown! The best decisions are made through prayer." God was continuing to shape and mold her as much as He was me. I'm eternally thankful for that!

There is so much I could share with you about this woman of God. But I really want you to get to the reason why you now hold this book. It's not my words, but the words spoken by Sonya. She is my wife, a mother, daughter, pastor, teacher, author, and a friend. I'll leave you with this final thought.

Soon after our journey together began, I learned Sonya was very adept at what can only be known as "Sonyaism's!" They are, in a nutshell, phrases or statements that are uniquely Sonya. One of the very first she shared with me was, "I don't ever wake up to lose!" Wow, what a winning way to live life! As Sonya's husband, I can tell you that you will want to find your favorite reading spot, your favorite blanket, and a new box of Kleenex. As you read each chapter, you may be able to find similarities that you can relate to. Parts of her journey that are like your own. Some may make you laugh; some may make you cry. Some will make you think, but her heart's desire is to in some way, help to make you whole. Be blessed!

INTRODUCTION

Inside of each person is a story. A story that includes the highs and lows of life, hardships, turns and twists, fairytales and make-believe, plots that are built with villains and heroes, yet many stories still lie buried inside a person's soul, never told because they are too painful to be exposed.

My name is Sonya Dorothy Wright. I am a native of Brooklyn, New York, a wife, mother, daughter, sister, teacher, Minister of The Gospel of Jesus Christ, and a friend, and I have a story to share with you.

CHAPTER 1

Broken But Not Defeated

"I put my pain to ink and wrote my peace."

Although it's true that time heals all wounds, the process it takes to journey through your grief and suffering to reach recovery can be just as traumatic. I've gone through more heartbreaking things than I ever imagined I could handle. I'm sure I'm not the only one among many of you who have gone through heartbreak after heartbreak and spent years dealing with regret, excruciating guilt, shame, and rejection, as well as occasionally wrestling with the idea of giving up. Sometimes life throws us an unexpected curveball that knocks the wind out of us and we find ourselves seeking support from our fellow Christian brothers and sisters in church, but instead we are greeted with unhealed broken vessels discipling others from an empty cup.

When the Lord asked me to devote my life to full-time ministry, I cried, and I cried because I knew the path that I would travel would be difficult. I was afraid and I had feelings of inadequacy. I frequently did the opposite of what the Lord was asking of me, but this time was different. My spirit had already said yes to the Lord. I had a strong desire to get out of the boat and be obedient to the Lord even though I knew that there would be times of loneliness, rejection, persecution, and suffering. My heart also understood that the Lord had called and chosen me to be His hands and feet and that He had not called me to fit in. He called me to be different, to be set apart, to go to places that no one else would want to go, and most importantly, that He would be with me no matter where He sent me. Therefore, despite how I felt, I made the decision to follow the Lord and rely on His strength for the difficult, but ultimately fulfilling and life-changing adventure that lay ahead.

Long before I answered my calling, God had already chosen me as an ordained Minister of the Gospel of Jesus Christ. I was commissioned in 2017 and held a few pastoral positions within this religious organization. Throughout my four and a half years as a pastor, I worked with other leaders and pastors who were spiritually toxic, abusive in their spiritual conduct toward their church and staff and abused their authority. They exploited their position of spiritual influence in ways that are unimaginable for those who are blood-washed Believers. I experienced emotional and spiritual abuse while serving as a pastor in a religious organization. However, God knew that my experiences would not destroy me, but instead help shape and mold me into the person I have become today. I want to make it clear that it wasn't the congregation members I served; rather, it was the organization's leadership. I should add that not all my leadership experiences were negative; nonetheless, the ones I had overshadowed the ones that were intended to edify and strengthen God's people.

It really can feel as if the rug has been pulled out from under you when you experience spiritual abuse or rejection from the church. Giving up my church home of over a decade and losing my community all at once was what it meant for me to step away from my position. It felt both alienating and traumatic. Even though this season of my life is over, this part of my story has nevertheless taught me a lot of valuable lessons, one is which can be found in God's Word and is embedded in my heart, "This is what the Sovereign Lord says: I am against the shepherds and will hold them accountable for my flock." (Ez. 34:10a)

I believe that spiritual abuse is one of the many reasons why there are so many wounded soldiers in the Body of Christ. We live in such an age where people are wandering aimlessly to find something to give meaning to life. They are hungry and thirsty because the weight of the world is squeezing the life out of them, and the church has the solution. We have the answer to feed and satisfy their hunger and thirst and that is JESUS. Sadly, there are far too many spiritually wounded pastors who have mastered the skill of abusing their flock while ministering to God's people. They allow their church to bear the brunt of their brokenness, which has a horrible impact on individuals who need to know about the unconditional love of Jesus Christ.

The one thing that I believe to be the most harmful about spiritually wounded leaders is that often, these leaders lead from an unresolved place and unintentionally or knowingly do harm to others. The effects of spiritual abuse sent me on a spiritual roller-coaster of negative feelings that made me doubt my value and worth, causing me to experience depression, anxiety, and other unhealthy emotions. It's true that "hurt people hurt people," but we can choose to be healed and transform into "healed people heal people" rather than staying in our hurt.

My darkest ministry experiences throughout my time in this organization included harassment, discrimination, and a toxic ministry atmosphere from leadership that left me feeling alone, rejected, and uncared for by individuals that I trusted and highly respected to love, support, lead, and guide me. I felt unheard and unseen.

One experience I can remember was when the Senior Pastors asked to meet with me following a revival, I led at my church that they were unimpressed with because people were praying in tongues. During the meeting they questioned me about my denominational background and what knowledge I had of other faith-based denominations that attended the revival. I responded by saying they are our brothers and sisters.

They proceeded to ask me who told me to do such a revival. I responded, "The Lord." I also shared that one of the young adults in the community wanted to do something to bring the churches together in the community, so he shared his vision of a "Worship Experience Night", and we partnered to do this amazing revival that was filled with believers from different denominations that was under one roof lifting the name of Jesus. It was the most beautiful worship experience I had ever seen. The Senior

Pastors told me that I could never have a revival like that again with people speaking in tongues and any revivals going forward must be the style of worship based on this religious organization.

After my meeting with my Senior Pastors, I contacted my Divisional Leaders and requested a meeting with them to discuss the meeting I had with my Senior Pastors, and they also agreed with what they had instructed me to do. I was so disappointed and hurt by my leadership because I felt they were wrong. How can we preach that we love inclusively but exclude other faith-based groups because the way they worship looks different. None of this made sense to me but I submitted to my organization's orders and never did a revival again. I continued to be mistreated and later wrote a grievance letter to the Divisional Headquarters, but I never received a response, even to this day.

I can write an entire book on all the lessons the Lord has taught me through each difficult and painful church experience I had in this organization. I believe in sharing this portion of my life; it has been part of my healing, helping others to know they are not alone. I am also very thankful for the many spiritual giants that spoke life into me when I was weary of doing well-doing, when I felt broken beyond repair. I believe they were my angels that stood in the gap for me. I had so much pain and trauma from leadership that I contemplated walking away from the ministry all together, but God had other plans. When I could not pray for myself, when I wanted to give up, and I felt like I was losing my mind, these brothers and sisters came to the pit in which I lied hopeless and defeated and loved me past my pain. They listened without judgment and walked alongside me and reminded me of who I was and whom I belong to.

When people ask me how I learned to love so well, my response is because I had to learn how to forgive. I never anticipated being so hurt by the church, but I've come to see that the Lord was teaching me what not to do in ministry during that season of hurt. How not to treat people so I would know how to treat people. How to love all people inclusively. How to extend forgiveness just as Christ does. I also learned the difference between someone who hurts and someone who heals. Out of their own suffering, someone who is struggling hurts others. Someone who has accepted God's healing imparts healing to others.

One insightful quote I came across by Iyanla Vanzant, an American motivational speaker, author, lawyer, and life coach, that really spoke to me was "True freedom is giving people permission to misunderstand you. In any situation, you have the power and ability to choose your experience." When people misunderstand you, let them. Don't argue with those committed to misunderstanding you.

We strengthen our faith when we decide to let God help us overcome our hurt by loving those who have wronged us. Our spiritual maturity is measured by our ability to feed on God's Word, to see the various ways Jesus expresses His love for us, and to grow up!

Consider reading God's Word if dealing with tough individuals is difficult for you. Jesus says in Luke 6:32, *"What credit do you get for loving those who love you?"* In Luke 6:35, Jesus challenges His people to love their enemies and do good to them. It is not enough to love those who are easy to love; we must also love those who are hard to love. God requires us to love everyone, even those who mistreat and misunderstand us; we do not get to choose who deserves God's love.

I realized that everything I had gone through had been beneficial to me. I was uncomfortable with the ways God was stretching me, but He knew it was necessary for me to learn what unconditional love meant. The Lord also desired to demonstrate to me that my identity, value, and worth came solely from Christ and had nothing to do with my title or the opinions of others. Never let someone else's perception of you influence how you see yourself. Never forget who you are or whose you belong too!

As children of God, we cannot stay where we are and grow in God. Any unhealthy relationship stunts our growth, even the one we have with ourselves. Growth is immeasurable and looks different in every person and oftentimes it is birthed out of brokenness. Brokenness is the catalyst to rebirth in which the Lord does the work by alluring us into places that oftentimes bring unpredictable pain that only He can heal. But we get to choose healing over hurting.

We get to choose to allow the Master Physician to heal our hearts only as He can and become whole in Christ. There is nothing that we will ever experience in this lifetime that is too hard for God and because God's Spirit lives within each of us, we have the strength to overcome defeat. We may experience times of brokenness in our life, but we are never defeated. We can either choose to trust God to get us through it, so that we can be ministers of reconciliation or we can choose to hold on to hurt, unforgiveness, and bitterness until we become someone who hurts others.

I don't know about you, but I am choosing to be a minister of reconciliation to share in the suffering of Christ who promised to be with us, share in glory, and have an abundance of His comfort. Don't allow your hurt to hinder your healing. Do the work that needs to be done for your personal healing. It will be good for your soul and a witness to others that healing is necessary for self-discovery.

Now if we are children, then we are heirs—heirs of God and co-heirs with Christ, if indeed we share in his sufferings in order that we may also share in his glory.

Romans 8:17:

Now if we are children, then we are heirs—heirs of God and co-heirs with Christ, if indeed we share in his sufferings in order that we may also share in his glory.

CHAPTER 2

Courage is Not a Picture

"When no one else is willing to stand with you,
have the courage to stand alone."

Courage in the darkest moments of your life makes you stronger. It brings about an inner strength and bravery that you never knew you had. Courage, in my opinion, is what makes individuals resilient, gives us the strength to go through open doors, and gives us the will to speak up and live the free lives that God intended for us.

One of my favorite quotes written by Eleanor Roosevelt is, "Courage is more exhilarating than fear and in the long run, it is easier. We do not have to become heroes overnight. Just one step at a time, meeting each thing that comes up, seeing it is not as dreadful as it appeared, discovering we have the strength to stare it down."

Growing up in Brooklyn, you needed courage because those concrete jungle streets would eat you alive if you weren't courageous. However, I wasn't always courageous, and certainly never saw myself as a courageous person as a child. I was quite fearful of everything but dared to try everything, I guess that was the kid in me. My mother would tell me, "If you keep playing with fire, you're going to get burnt."

Needless to say, my mom was right. I got burnt repeatedly but it never quenched my curiosity. Although my inquisitiveness compelled me "to walk on coals" as a child, I was doing it just as timidly as I could. And just in case you are thinking, "Did she really walk on coals?" Absolutely not!

It was easy for me to play it safe and hide behind my fears as a child. My atmosphere and reality stifled me rather than encouraged me to be bold. When I watched television, I used to imagine what my life would be like if I were one of the actors. I often had the impression that I was an outsider in my own body, living two separate lives—one in my dreams and the other in the real world.

I was fearful of so many things for so many reasons. Fearful of being rejected, fearful of failing, fearful of people finding out that I didn't know everything, fearful that people wouldn't accept me for me. I spent most of my life being a counterfeit. I looked like I had it all together, but I was really pretending, hiding behind my own shadow of insecurities. It's crazy how the enemy can use fear to keep you from being who God has created you to be until you realize the very thing you were afraid of is the very thing God uses to transform your life and the lives of those you encounter.

Knowing what I know now, I would tell my younger self, be bold, be brave, be courageous. It's totally okay to spread your wings, it's ok to feel disappointment, it's okay to make mistakes but always get back up and never give up on yourself! I repeat, *never give up on yourself!*

There is a warrior on the inside of you that was created fearfully, and wonderfully made (Psalm 139:14), and God himself is with you. Yes, you will feel strength and as you start walking on this path, it will be hard. Growth is hard. Change is hard. But nothing is as hard as staying some-where that you simply no longer belong. It takes courage to move forward and do something different, and with God's help, you can do it.

In this game called life, you will get the wind knocked out of you. You will feel hopeless and defeated at times, but it is during these times that you will come to the revelation of how strong and courageous you really are, if you don't give up. There is victory on the other side of the storm.

You can choose to think about all the things that went wrong in your life, or you can choose to thank God for all the lessons learned that made you stronger. Having courage is a choice, and when the opportunity presents itself, we get to choose to be courageous or comfortable.

Our failures are meant to teach us who we are. They are meant to show us not to give up on ourselves and God. Trust that God has a plan for your life and the failure and rejections you have experienced are not meant to destroy but are meant to build your character. Trust God even when you don't understand or when you can't hear His voice. Be obedient and remain faithful. The Lord has the blueprint for your life.

Life has a way of teaching us lessons, and as we get older, we realize the lessons and experiences helped shape and mold us to become who we are today. It is through these life lessons that we get to embrace courage and see things from a different perspective. Our perspective may be clouded if we are afraid that we may lose everything, and it can be frightening to think that having courage will cost you everything. But it might be the only thing separating you from your destiny. Get out of the boat! You may not be the greatest swimmer, or you may not know how to swim at all, but the purpose of getting out the boat is not about you knowing how to swim so you won't sink but it is keeping your focus on Jesus, the One that keeps you from sinking.

In terms of courage, there are three things I've discovered. "Life is happening for you, not to you." Everything we go through and have experienced in life is purposeful. We should never be moved by the things we see but be moved by what God is doing in what we cannot see. He will get the glory out of it. Never waste time fighting a battle that belongs to God. Our job is to be obedient to God. Be a willing and available vessel so that He can use you to show others who He is. You have already achieved victory because of what Christ did at Calvary. He is just using you as a vessel and you have everything you need on the inside to overcome any obstacle or trial you may be facing. We get to be the hands and feet of Jesus and partner with Him and share with others how to overcome.

Anything that you accomplish outside of yourself will require courage. It will require God's strength to navigate from complexity to new waters that will test you beyond your limits, but in the end, the Lord will be glorified, and you will be better for it.

So don't allow the things that set you back to define you. See them as a learning experience placed in your path to teach you something you didn't know about yourself. You are not defined by your past. You are defined by the One who holds your future in His hands. Your setback prepares you for a great comeback and God's timing is perfect! Can I get an Amen!

It took courage for me to be the mother of two incredible young women. I wasn't the perfect mother. Many of the poor decisions I made affected them, and my mistakes served as teaching opportunities for them. As parents, we must acknowledge that we are the primary role models for our children and that they will imitate the lessons we teach them. My girls needed to see me as the virtuous woman God has called me to be, and I knew deep down that I needed the courage to change and face my fears and trust God. I am grateful that God revealed to me what He had already been working on inside of me before I even realized it, and that my mistakes have not changed His plans for my beautiful daughters, Rudy, and Faith, who are each on their own spiritual journey with the Lord and are destined for greatness, because God said so!

The second valuable lesson I learned about courage is to "make life simple." My life was spiraling out of control. I was living beneath the standard of God, and I willfully forfeited my right as an heir to the King of Kings and Lord of Lords. I went to church regularly, but I didn't have a relationship with God. In other words, I was a bench warmer. I sat in the pews, but I never got in the game. My thoughts were all over the place and my heart was polluted with the chaos that was happening in my mind. Suicidal thoughts, anxiety, and depression became a norm for me. I didn't realize how lost I was until I hit rock bottom. My picture-perfect life all came crashing down and as I watched it unfold, it made me think how I had allowed myself to get it here. The red flags, the warnings, and wise councils, I ignored them all. It wasn't until then that I began to crawl my way out of the hole into which I dug myself.

The Lord showed me kindness and reminded me of who I was in Him. He showed me the queen I had never seen in the mirror. I can remember the Holy Spirit speaking to me and saying, "If you don't live for me, you will surely die." This terrified me because I knew better but I allowed the enemy to fool me, to think that stuff and bad relationships would be better. And they weren't. I began the long journey of decluttering my life from people, bad habits, and stinking. I fell in love with God all over again but this time, it was different. I was chasing after Him because I desperately wanted the peace of God that surpasses all understanding (Philippians 4:7).

When we simplify our lives, we liberate ourselves from the unrealistic expectations of life. When we are overwhelmed and burdened by the troubles of this life, our emotions tend to get the best of us. We are burdened by carrying unrealistic expectations. We frequently value our lives based on what we do. We feel the pressure of being a fixer and the burden of worrying instead of praying.

Jesus invites His children to cast their cares on Him: "Come to me, all you who are weary and burdened, and I will give you rest. Take my yoke upon you and learn from me, for I am gentle and humble in heart, and you will find rest for your souls. For my yoke is easy and my burden is light." (Matthew 11:28–30).

Unrealistic expectations are something you can never keep up with. There are undercurrents of failure when unrealistic demands are made. Therefore, resist letting other people's unreasonable expectations run berserk in your life. Decide instead to base your choices on what is practical rather than on trying to win someone over or impress them. Rather than being a people pleaser, be a God pleaser. Make life simple for your future self, and learn to obey God above all else, and your future self will be better for it.

My third lesson. "Courage is one step at a time, one moment at a time." Just like life isn't a sprint, courage is not always a huge step. You can only face the storms of life by practicing trust in Jesus against the chaos of everyday life. You can overcome your fears by having faith in God. In God's Word, we can find countless stories of how God used ordinary people like you and me and oftentimes, fearful people to do great things that saved the lives of many people. Moses, after fleeing Egypt and spending years away, faced his insecurities and fears by responding to God's call to go back to the very place in which his fears began. He was motivated by God's vision of working through him to save his people, the Jews, from the suffering they were experiencing.

Queen Esther's story changed my life. God will put you in the right place at the right time. His time! Queen Esther had reached a crossroad in her faith. She was a Jewish woman who was chosen to be the new Queen of Persia and wife of the King of Persia, where many Jews lived. A few years later, a man named Haman, a high official in the king's court, decided to kill all the Jews—all because of one Jewish man who wouldn't bow down to him. That man was Mordecai, Esther's cousin. Mordecai begged Esther to help. But that meant going to the king, and she could have been killed for doing that without permission. The Queen had a choice to make that would impact the lives of her people. Would she dare to stand up for the Lord and His chosen people? Or would she just blend into society as Persian royalty?

God made a way out of no way. He made sure the king was happy to see Esther when she came. Esther and Mordecai were able to save their people, but only because God planned everything perfectly. He put them where they needed to be. He gave them courage and wisdom. God can't always be seen, but He is always working for the good of His people.

Just as God gave Queen Esther the strength to be courageous, He will do the same for us. The question is, are you willing to respond to God's calling? Serving God often demands that we risk our own security. We must choose to be courageous and take a stand for God. When we do, lives will be changed.

God is not pleased with a humility that rejects obedience to Him. Do what God tells you to do! It costs you everything, but you will gain so much more than you lost. Don't allow your fears to cause you to react in disbelief. Instead, take it one day at a time. One disciplined step at a time! One better choice at a time and soon you will see a new and transformed you! Don't fake it to make it! Faith it to make it!

Never minimize yourself or feel bad about your personal growth to make someone else feel good about themselves. There are some people that may never see or acknowledge your growth, but they don't know what you have overcome, nor the trials and tribulations you have faced and how the Lord delivered you out of every situation. They don't know the many nights you prayed to the Lord in your season of waiting that you were in when the Lord was silent. Because the Lord has done and is still doing wonderful things, don't be ashamed to proclaim His goodness.

Those that know and love you will be by your side through good and bad times. They are the ones that you may not speak to every day but are cheering you on because they know what you have done, and they are genuinely happy for you. I share all of this to say, be about your Father's business and be the light of Jesus!

Joshua 1:9

"Have I not commanded you? Be strong and courageous. Do not be afraid; do not be discouraged, for the Lord your God will be with you wherever you go."

CHAPTER 3

Suffering With a Purpose

*"There is nothing more agonizing than suffering without cause
than suffering. A great deal of us have gone through the death of a loved
one, experiencing intolerable and almost paralyzing sadness. But it was
through that grief that we discovered suffering with a purpose."*

The day my entire world changed was March 7, 1992. My dear husband, whom I had first met when I was in high school, was killed on this day. At the time of his passing, I was twenty-two years old and seven-and-a-half months pregnant with our daughter Rudy. I was completely devastated when my husband unexpectedly passed away. No words can adequately express how I felt when I hurried to the hospital after learning that Rudolph had been shot and the doctor, who had attempted to save his life, informed me that my husband had not survived.

I screamed "NO!" into Heaven's ear as I collapsed to the ground. I was sobbing excessively when the nurses arrived—they didn't want me to go into early labor. I can still picture the nurses helping me up off the floor and giving me oxygen because I was having trouble breathing. There was nothing anyone could have done to change what I had just heard, which had become my worst nightmare.

I suddenly found myself a widow and a single mother. I was hurt, upset, depressed, and completely broken. The man I believed I would spend my entire life with and help raise our daughter—the love of my life—left me in an instant. My entire body became numb, and I felt as though I had passed away beside him in the hospital. The shock of my husband's death brought with it all the questions, "Why did this happen?", "How am I going to survive without my husband?", "Is this really happening?", "How am I going to make it?", "How am I going to raise our daughter without her father?", "How do I live after such a traumatic experience?" and "Why did God allow this to happen?"

The sudden death of my spouse was the most horrific event I have ever experienced that caused great pain and suffering upon me and those who knew him. It was also the moment I understood that death owes no one an explanation. Death does not make distinctions. Death is inescapable and does not care about who you are, how much money you have or do not have, or how firmly you believe in God or not. This is why it is imperative for every one of us to be ready for the day the Lord summons us home and to rejoice in the knowledge that He has prepared a place for those who have confessed Him as Lord and Savior.

Everything about that experience haunted me for years. I replayed every moment in my mind repeatedly to try and make some sense of what was happening. I remember what he was wearing, the joyful mood he was in, and the last words we exchanged before he died was me asking him to pick me up some butter pecan ice cream, which he always did when he was out because he knew it was my favorite craving. I said, "I love you," and him replied with, "I love you too, and I'll be back." Little did I know that he would never be back; he would be gone forever.

Both Rudolph and I grew up in Brooklyn, New York, also known as the "concrete jungle." "Because of the violence and drugs that were rampant in our neighborhood, it was tough to grow up in the East New York borough, where he lived in Cypress Projects, and I lived on Liberty Avenue. I loved growing up in Brooklyn. I loved my family and friends, the block parties, summer jams, they were some of the best times of my life. Brooklyn is where I learned how to survive. It was where I met the man that God would use to be part of my story.

Rudolph and I met on the "A" train on my way home from school. I can still clearly recall that day. I was listening to Cameo's *Just Like Candy*, on my Walkman, and he came over to where I was sitting and asked me what I was listening to. I told him, and he asked if he could listen, so I let him. My friends and I started laughing as he started to dance. He proceeded to tell me his name "Taheem," which was his nickname or otherwise known as his street name, and then asked me what my name was and if he could have my phone number and I said yes. I never liked calling him by his street name, so I called him by his birth name "Rudolph,"—only his family was allowed to call him by that name.

Rudolph was charming, funny, creative, and kind. He was a well-known rap musician in New York and enjoyed rap music. His goal was to become a successful rap musician so he could support his family. He had a strong determination and would finish whatever he set his mind to. Rudolph was tenacious in his pursuit of success. He was incredibly smart. He was very concerned about taking care of the people he loved, especially his family and friends. He was not a flawless man. He had a troubled life. His mother was a very kind woman who was facing her own troubles, and his father was dead, and he had never met him. So, I met a man that was troubled and had a dark side that would later be revealed to me.

At the time we met, I did not know his means of income; I did not know he was a drug dealer, but I had a sense that he lived a flashy life because of all the expensive jewelry and designer clothing he wore, which made me wonder how he was able to afford all these things. I was a bit naive for sixteen years old. I was a church girl, a straight A student working at McDonald's. I never asked him any questions about how he earned his income. I just assumed he was getting paid well at his job. After a few months of dating, we fell in love. My mother did not agree with me having a boyfriend at sixteen, especially Rudolph. She felt he was no good for me and she did not like him. I was not allowed to see him, so I snuck behind her back. We continued dating and I slowly began to change.

Rudolph later shared with me that he was a drug dealer, which I knew was wrong, but I had accepted his lifestyle because I loved him. By the age of seventeen, I lost my virginity, became pregnant, and miscarried in McDonald's bathroom. I was becoming someone I did not recognize, all in the name of love. Rudolph had been in and out of jail during the time we dated and by the time I graduated from high school, he was sentenced to three years in prison. You would have thought that I would have left him and gone on with my life, but I didn't. I chose to stand by the man that I loved. During the three years while Rudolph was in prison, I worked hard pursuing my career in finance. I visited him quite often and prayed that he would be a changed man when he was released. And when he asked me to marry him during his incarceration, I said yes. We eloped on February 28, 1990, because I knew my mother would not have approved of me marrying him.

Rudolph was released from prison in June 1991, started working, and everything was going well. When I became pregnant in August 1991, Rudolph decided that he was going back to his old lifestyle of drug dealing. I was so hurt because I knew that if he chose this route, he would either die or go back to jail. I had even expressed how I felt about his decision, and he still was adamant about this being his only option because he wanted to provide the best for his child. My heart was broken. Rudolph had a promising rap career that was going to take off and job with benefits, but he chose to take the biggest risk. He was not afraid be afraid of the consequences that could potentially happen that would impact the lives of those who loved him, especially his unborn child.

Our relationship suffered when he made the decision to go back to his previous way of life. He started being physically aggressive when we got into an argument. I became fearful that he was going to seriously hurt our unborn child and I left him numerous times. But each time, he would call and apologize, and I would return. I didn't even recognize the person I had become, and I hated looking into the mirror. My self-esteem was gone. When I looked into his eyes, I couldn't see the man I initially met in high school—the kind, caring, and gentle soul—finding his way back home. All I saw was a broken, scared man full of anger. I no longer recognized him and that was the most painful part about watching someone you love spiral down a dark path and there was nothing you could do about it but pray.

Rudolph's poor decisions put us in danger. Drugs and weapons were everywhere in our house. I avoided my mother and my other relatives out of fear and shame for who I had become. I knew better because my mother had raised me better. I was a disgrace and a shame to my family, but I felt stuck and was not strong enough to leave. Although I was unaware of it at the time, the Lord had undoubtedly been keeping an eye on me the night Rudolph died. It was the end of one life and the start of a new one for me.

It has been thirty years since Rudolph's death, and I am a living witness of God's amazing grace. My daughter and I could have both lost our lives, but the Lord spared our lives. I made many poor decisions and held God accountable for many years because I did not know how to process my pain and suffering, but God was patient with me and healed my heart. When the Lord remained silent when I needed to know why, He gave me the strength and peace to trust in Him and move on. Although Rudolph and I both grew up in the church and were aware of the wrongness of our lifestyles, I never considered the repercussions of living a life outside of God's Will, but God gave me a second chance. The Lord never gave up on me.

This world may believe that God causes calamity and suffering upon His people because He allows these things to happen. Bad things, unfortunately, do happen to good people. Bad things happen because we live in a fallen world. The saved, and the unsaved, occupy the same space on this earth, but we are not of this world (John 17:16).

Satan wants us to believe that when we are prospering, we will not suffer, but that is not true (2 Timothy 3:12). Our family and friends may believe our sufferings may be God's way of judging our sins, but this is not always true (1 Peter 3:18). Suffering is God's way to teach, refine, and strengthen our faith in Him. Suffering allows God to shape and mold us into the people He has called us to be. Suffering causes us to discipline our minds by making us focus our hope on the grace to be revealed at the revelation of Jesus Christ (1 Pet 1:6, 13). It is our responsibility, as

Christians, to always keep our eyes on Jesus, through the good and bad times. We must continue to confess our sins to God and call on Him alone for strength. Refrain from self-pity and seek God for understanding and help. We should be open to receive support from fellow believers who can encourage us through difficult times. Lastly, we need to draw nearer to God and proclaim our faith to Him, believing that He cares and waits patiently for us.

CHAPTER 4

God's Timing is Perfect

"When we learn to wait for God's timing, we realize
that He was there all along."

Even as a grown person, I felt the effects of being a fatherless daughter. I spent so many years looking for love in all the wrong places. Then love showed up as a counterfeit, a wolf in sheep's clothing. I thought I was marrying a man of God, but he wasn't that at all and he took advantage of my weakness and vulnerability.

I was married to a person that was very abusive. I didn't know that at the very beginning. He was a church-going person, a loving person, and I didn't realize that I was in a "sleeping with the enemy" situation until he had a bi-polar episode. That was the moment I realized that I was in serious trouble. That's also when his family confessed to me that he had bi-polar disorder. Had I known, I wouldn't have gotten involved with this man, especially as the mother of two young daughters.

I stayed in an abusive marriage for over eight years, unable to leave until I began a cleaning contract at a church. Ironically, it was this same church that would later become the source of more abuse and frustration. But in the beginning, it was my refuge and my safety.

Toward the end of my marriage, I remember one of the pastors saying to me, "Your walk is not authentic."

I looked at her and thought, "Who do you think you are, lady?" And the Holy Spirit kept telling me, "Shut up. Listen to her."

She said to me, "You come to church one way, but you go home another way."

In that moment, I started crying and I asked, "How do you know this? How do you know?"

She said, "Because I was once you. I don't know when you're going to leave or how you're going to leave, but God is going to make a way of escape for you."

I stayed in that relationship for several years after that conversation. When I finally left, though, she encouraged me to stay in the ministry. Her church had a program that served women coming out of sexual exploitation and sex trafficking in that area and she wanted me to minister to those women.

I was shocked. Me? She wanted me, the faker, the pretender, to minister to these women who had already suffered so much. But she told me that I was the perfect person to work with them because of what I'd gone through. And she was so right. God used my brokenness in that ministry to deliver me.

Sometimes you don't understand that God uses your brokenness to deliver you. One day we were right in the middle of doing a Bible study with the women, and I started ministering to them. I felt the Lord tell me to confess to them what I was going through, and I started telling them about my situation. I said, "Ladies, what you don't know right now is that I'm going through an abusive relationship. My lights are out. I haven't seen him in a few days. There's no food in my house."

At that point, even my daughters left me. My oldest daughter Rudy looked at me and said, "Mommy, if you aren't going to save yourself, I'm going to save my sister and I." When they left, my youngest daughter was thirteen years old, and Rudy was twenty years old. Faith went to live with her father, while Rudy went to live with my mother in Richmond, Virginia.

When my daughters left, I felt hopeless because I abandoned them. I had to live with the guilt of knowing that I'd chosen a man over my children.

Yet even in the moment my daughters decided to leave, the Holy Spirit told me to let them go. In my soul, I knew that if I didn't, something bad would happen to them. In fact, years later, my daughter told me that he tried to assault her. She had the courage that I didn't have, not only to save herself, but to save her little sister. They flew away, and there I stayed in that abusive relationship. But all along, God was watching over me.

I remember during this time; I kept praying to God and asking him to send me a sign to leave my marriage. I was so desperate for the Lord to release me from this man. And you know what God said to me?

"I didn't tell you to marry him in the first place!"

Just before the end of my marriage, I had the beautiful opportunity to go on a mission trip to India. There, the Lord spoke to me and told me I was called to full-time ministry. I thought, "God, you've got to be kidding me! Nobody is going to listen to me. Do you not see what I'm dealing with right now? I am a wayward woman. Who's going to listen to me, Jesus?"

He said, "They're not listening to you, they're listening to me."

During that trip, I was ministering to women in the Red-Light District. There was one woman I met who'd lost her husband. She told me that the only way she could make money was to sell her body. My church paid thousands of dollars to get her off the street and away from her pimp, and I was so amazed at the work of the church at the time. For better or for worse, I said "yes" to God, inspired and amazed by what I'd seen, and on fire to make a difference in the world.

Yet still I knew I was unequally yoked to a man who didn't want to do anything productive with his life, let alone go into full-time ministry, and who was regularly harming me physically and mentally.

Unfortunately, I kept going back to him time and time again. It wasn't until his therapist called, not looking for him but looking for me. He said to me, "I'm very concerned about you. If you don't leave him, he's going to kill you and get away with it. He's mentally ill and he doesn't want to stay on his medication."

In that moment, the Lord blessed my godmother's soul, and she told me, "You are leaving there. As soon as you get your income tax check, we're going down to the courthouse and we're filing for divorce."

After that, I stayed with her for a while, and in that time, I continued to follow the Lord's leading in my life and started the process of entering the ministry. In the process of finalizing my divorce, the church sent me to another location to serve as a church assistant until I could be accepted into their seminary.

You already know that things didn't turn out like I'd hoped. There were so many unexpected challenges, including even more abuse, this time spiritually. There were deep moments of racism and exploitation that I could have never anticipated. How could a church that spent thousands of dollars to rescue a prostitute from her pimp in India be the same church that continued to tell me that I would never be good enough as I was?

For nearly four years I endured their abuse, until I'd finally had enough. I was living in Biloxi, MS, and had surrounded myself with a community of strong and amazing women of God. I took the time I needed to heal from what I'd been put through as a minister, when leaders from my church who'd been moved to Chicago started telling me about a position there.

I told them that the position sounded wonderful, but I didn't have it in me to be in full-time ministry. I would be happy to take the position as a lay person, as it aligned perfectly with my beliefs and passions, but I would not do it with "Pastor" in front of my name.

They agreed, and I left the warm embrace of my community for the cold of the unknown. It was an unexpectedly hard season. I'd left everything I'd known and was in a place unfamiliar to me. Those same leaders started putting pressure on me to reenter the ministry, telling me how gifted I was and how the church needed more leaders like me. Foolishly, I believed them, and in a way, my decision to go back into the ministry was made from trauma.

I wanted that community of believers back. I wanted to feel the warm embrace of people who loved me again. That's what they were offering, or so it seemed. I knew my abuser, and went back, just like I had in my marriage. So far in my life, it was the one thing I knew how to do well. I didn't have the tools or the resources to keep pushing forward. I was at a crossroads, facing going back to the trauma I knew or having the strength to move forward. I lacked the strength, so I decided to go back. It's so painful to go forward into the unknown.

The second time I shouldn't have gone back. Although I did it, God used it. Because sometimes we do things and we think it's God, but God allows it. Everything has a purpose, and the Lord used it anyway. I had friends tell me that I shouldn't go back, but it all had to do with pride. I felt like I wanted to be loyal to people for all they'd done for me, meanwhile God was sending me all kinds of stop signs and yield signs saying, "You don't have to do this." And I did it anyway.

Throughout my life, I always got the timing wrong. Yet God's timing was still perfect. He used my imperfect timing as an opportunity for his timing to be perfect. In the midst of going back into full-time ministry in this religious organization, I still had other ministries that I had established on my own, and I was very upfront with my church that I intended to keep doing these ministries.

One such ministry (that I still do today) is called The Gospel Tea Talks. It's an online platform where I have candid conversations with ordinary people who are doing extraordinary things one faith step at a time. I met my dear friend, Dr. Yolanda Henderson, who is an amazing woman of God in Biloxi, MS in 2019.God used her to be the catalyst to help me step out of my comfort zone. When I felt fearful of the unknown, she would always tell me to "Do It Afraid", and so I did. I faced my fears and trusted God to do the rest.

October 2021, I was a special guest on her church broadcast in honor of Domestic Violence Awareness month. I had no idea that her best friend was the man who would end up becoming my husband. Every time she mentioned her "best friend," I always pictured a female. It never dawned on me that he was a man, let alone the man God had for me.

The broadcast was entitled *"Love Doesn't Hurt"* in honor of domestic violence. She also invited her best friend, Lee Wright, to offer a male perspective. I spent the show spilling all my dirty laundry, and Lee heard everything about all the abuse I had gone through in past relationships. He just listened and never said anything other than, "Men, we need to speak up and protect women."

After the show, when we were all in the virtual green room, she said, "Who knows, maybe your Boaz is right here!" I had no idea what she was talking about. I wasn't even thinking about Lee in that way, nor was I actively looking for a relationship. We left the greenroom, and I immediately called her to ask her what she was talking about.

She said, "I think you and Lee should be *friends.*"

I responded with such pride, "Girl, I'm good."

She told me, "I bet he's going to send you an instant message."

I was willing to bet he wouldn't, but it was a bet I would have lost. Sure enough, he did reach out to me, and we became good friends. He even came to Chicago to visit me.

Later he told me that he was content with his single life as well. He wasn't necessarily looking for a wife, but when he planned his trip to visit me, he prayed to the Lord to see my heart. He said, "God, I don't want to see what she looks like, I want to see her heart." And he told me that God showed him my heart. Neither of us were looking for anybody at that point in our lives, but it was God who brought us together.

I was single for eight years between my awful divorce and when I met my wonderful husband, my gift from God, Lee Andre Wright. In that time, I'd almost given up on ever finding romantic love again. I was content with myself and with my relationship with God. I was in a place where I didn't think that a man could add anything to the fulfilling life that I had. I had my fair share of bad relationships, and I wasn't interested in entertaining foolishness, nor raising a grown man or doing social work. I was over it and I was not willing to put myself back out there only to be hurt and disappointed again. Although I was content with my singleness, my desire to be loved and share a meaningful life with someone, who would treat me for the queen that I am, would not go away.

So, I prayed this prayer:

"Lord, if it is Your will for me to have a husband, I ask You, Lord, to bring this person that You have chosen for me into my life. I pray he has a heart that chases after You, that he is humble, caring, funny, handsome, smart, wise, organized, lives life on purpose and with purpose, strong but gentle, loves people and loves to serve You and others. And most of all, that he would honor, respect, care, cherish and love me for who I am. Also, that we would both help one another grow deeper in our relationship with You, Lord, and one another. When people see us, they will be encouraged by our union that belongs to You. In Jesus' Name."

Two months after praying this prayer, I met Lee, who was exactly the man I described to God. Only God could have brought us together.

If there's one thing I've learned in this life, it's that God is always right on time. Even when I've got it wrong, even when I've been disobedient and made decisions that have displeased him, he always makes a way for me and comes through right when I need him. God's timing is always perfect, even when we may feel impatient or forgotten.

Psalms 37:1-4

"Do not fret because of those who are evil or be envious of those who do wrong; for like the grass they will soon wither, like green plants they will soon die away. Trust in the Lord and do good; dwell in the land and enjoy safe pasture. Take delight in the Lord, and he will give you the desires of your heart."

God gave me the desires of my heart and for that I will be forever grateful. I had never experienced being in a relationship with someone who was not physically or emotionally abusive until I met Lee. For the first time in my life, I can truly say that I am loved by someone who cares for mind, body, and soul. Lee brings out the best version of me and most of all,

HE LOVES JESUS and serves Him and His people with all his heart—now that's a win!

For all the times my "picker" was broken, the Lord used this beautiful soul to open my heart to love. And what's so crazy about it all is that I was trying so desperately to push him away because I had so many trust issues. Sometimes we can think that we are healed from past trauma until we are triggered. Although my heart was yearning for a relationship, the hurt from previous relationships continued to influence my present. To protect myself from ever experiencing those emotions again, I built a wall. My wall is up, and it would take an act of God for my wall to come down. I remember at the beginning of our friendship; Lee had expressed interest in dating me and said these words during one of our deep conversations that opened my heart to receiving what God had for me. "Sonya, take the wall down so you can see."

On December 11, 2022, I married my lovely husband and best friend, Lee Andre Wright, who is my gift from God. It's been an amazing journey so far, and I feel grateful to God every day for giving me another opportunity to love and be loved. Our blended family of five children ranges in age from thirty-one to eight years old, and they keep us very busy, but we are grateful that God has chosen us to guide and teach them in His ways.

What's even more amazing is how God ordered our steps, and just when I believed full-time ministry was behind me, He called my husband and me to start a church. Elevation Worship Ministries International was birthed on January 1, 2023.

God has given us a vision and a mission to spread the Gospel of Jesus Christ and win souls in His name. We get to work alongside wonderful people who are passionate about reaching out to those who have been forgotten, rejected, abandoned and without hope. We get testify to God's faithfulness and redemption through the power of His blood, and "Together we are building a ministry without walls." Won't He Do It!

God's timing is perfect, not just for me but for all His children. In your waiting, pursue God. Pour your alabaster jar on the feet of Jesus. Lay it all before and surrender it all to Him.

CHAPTER 5

Winning Wounded

"Your wounds serve as a reminder of the battle that strengthened rather than destroyed you; they are a testament to your strength and courage."

I can remember the first wound I ever incurred. I was an adolescent, super hardheaded and knew it all. Whenever I was at the grocery store with my mother, she would always tell me not to swing on the pole because she feared that I would hurt myself, and like most kids, I would reassure my mother that I would listen and not swing on the pole—but as soon as she went into the store, guess who was swinging on the pole? Me! Needless to say, after repeated trips to the supermarket with my mother and swinging on the pole despite her warnings, my disobedience caught up with me and cost me a trip to the emergency room, where I received several stitches in the back of my head from swinging on the pole. My beautiful long hair had to be shaved, and I still have a bump in the back of my head as a reminder of that day.

It was my first wound, but it would certainly not be my last. I could easily write down every wound I ever got, how it happened, how it healed (or didn't heal), and what I learned from it. For now, I'll just say that my life covered me in wounds, and I didn't know how to make peace with them.

Until not long after I was ordained, I started experiencing terrible pain. I was bleeding a lot and had no idea what was going on with me. My doctor told me I needed to have an ultrasound, because until they could look inside me and see what was wrong, they wouldn't be able to diagnose the issue.

The ultrasound revealed huge cysts on my ovaries. They were the size of golf balls. And there wasn't just one or two, they were all over. My doctor recommended an emergency hysterectomy, because she couldn't tell if the cysts were cancerous or not. Even so, removing one cyst and doing a biopsy wouldn't fix the tremendous pain and bleeding I was experiencing. What was worse, if I didn't have the surgery, more cysts could continue to grow.

The surgery removed most of my reproductive organs, and it turned out that I had endometriosis. Had I not had the surgery, those cysts could have eventually turned cancerous and killed me. Even that knowledge didn't save me from the deep depression that followed.

My doctor recommended that I go to therapy. It was apparently very common for women who experienced a hysterectomy to go through depression. Imagine, women who go through this procedure lose all their reproductive organs and become very emotional. Our hormones can't balance the way they used to, and there's a deep feeling of loss.

It was my first time in therapy, and my therapist suggested a deep trauma therapy called Eye Movement Desensitization and Reprocessing (EMDR) to help me go back through my most painful moments in life and find healing. EMDR (Eye Movement Desensitization and Reprocessing) is a super painful, but ultimately rewarding form of therapy. I spent two years unraveling and un-layering several years of scars and pain that I didn't even realize were there.

She asked me, "When did this feeling of rejection and abandonment start?"

I told her, "It was at four when my dad left my mom. When he left her, he left us, too. He abandoned all of us. He was the first man who ever broke my heart."

He left a deep wound—a deep scar that I couldn't seem to move forward from. That was the catalyst for every bad relationship I ever had.

He set the example, the precedent for what I thought I should expect. I thought that every man would leave me, and no one would ever be willing to stay with me.

So, she told me to write a letter to my four-year-old self. She told me that that little four-year-old girl was part of my soul, still crying for attention. Now, I thought that was very weird. But then I was reminded that God can go back and talk to the parts of myself that are still broken. It's not weird to God. He's at the beginning and the end.

I began "speaking" to my four-year-old self in therapy, then wrote that letter. I was instructed to tell her all about myself. To tell her that I was sorry. Whatever I wanted and needed to say to tell her that she was valued and seen and okay and safe.

I thought it was cuckoo, I thought I was crazy, but let me tell you something. It was so healing. That little girl inside of me needed to know that she was okay. Here's what I wrote:

Hello My Beautiful Princess,

You are incredibly special to me, and I love you so much. I want you to know how much God loves you and that you are His precious daughter. In the Lord's eyes, you are perfect, and you are not a mistake. God is genuinely in love with you. Have faith in Him and rely on Him.

I want you to know that I deeply regret not setting a good example. I made a lot of stupid decisions that damaged you. Please forgive me. Please know that if I had known what I know now, I would have made different decisions.

Life will not be easy. Sometimes you will want to give up and consider suicide but keep going. Allow the tears and grief to flow so that all the hurt can be released from you. You'll adore it a lot. You will lose a lot, but every experience will improve you as a friend, mother, daughter, and person. Your mistakes don't define you; rather, they will help you develop as a person. Nothing you experience in life will be in vain. They will serve God's purposes.

Just like a flower, you will continue to grow.

Just like an eagle, you will continue to soar.

Just like a butterfly, you will continue to be unique.

Just like a rainbow, you will continue to be colorful.

A letter to my four-year-old self

I love you, little Sonya. Let's go be who God called us to be.

Then my therapist told me to write a letter to my teenage self. Then to my young adult self. I had to write a letter to every version of myself that had experienced hurt and trauma. All those parts of me that had been abused, they all needed to be healed and assured that they were safe.

Finally, I was able to put it all together and see the pattern of things I was using to validate my worth, that ultimately never could. And that was because I had not addressed the pain. And once I addressed the pain, and was honest with God about the pain, then the healing started to take place.

That's why I call this chapter "Winning Wounded," because I was very wounded in the pit of my soul from the age of four. Yet I was still winning along the way because God was still with me.

I think a lot of people don't understand that. You can be wounded and still win. Our wounds don't define us as failures. They're a reminder that we are very much victorious, that we don't just have to lay down and die.

When I was four, I was hurt by my dad who left me and my siblings. He rejected and abandoned us because he was dealing with his own issues and not ready to deal with the pressures of fatherhood. He didn't know who he was. So, I had to forgive him. He was a teenager who had children, so I couldn't continue to hold him hostage in my heart. I had to allow that wound to heal.

Oftentimes, I believe that unforgiveness is just unhealed wounds.

There are a lot of times I could have given in to that unforgiveness. I have experienced a lot of racism and discrimination in my life. One, I'm an African American woman, and two I live in a society where all women are underappreciated and undervalued. Putting those two together, we start to understand that the "privileges" of Black women are very low.

Even though I have many white sisters who would never treat me that way, but I can be in the middle of a room of white people who don't know me and never be noticed because of my skin. It makes me feel like my voice doesn't matter, and I must work that much harder just to keep up and make my voice heard.

That broke me a lot.

It also provoked me to always speak up for who I am and who God called me to be as a Black woman.

You would never believe the things that people have said to me. Then again, if you're a minority living in this country, you would not only believe it, but you've also probably experienced it yourself.

One of the most racist experiences I went through was when I worked at a bank in my early twenties. I majored in accounting and loved working in banks at the time. I was working in the back office, processing the trades that were going on. At the time, the company was experiencing layoffs.

The head trader of the desk came in and said to me, "You don't need to worry about anything, your Black ass isn't going anywhere. They need a token."

I was the only Black person in that department. It was a huge eye-opener for me. At the time, it shocked me, because he was someone, I always considered to be a brilliant, kind man. I wasn't going to do anything, but a good friend of mine told me, "You can't let that slide. If you do, he'll feel like he can say something else, and then something else. You must report him."

Of course, I didn't want to do that. I respected him, I thought he was my friend. But I did it anyway on the advice of my friend, and HR was livid. He was written up; they made him apologize to me; and they had a whole workshop about discrimination in the workplace. All because I spoke up. It was the first time I realized that I had a voice, and I could make a positive difference.

Mind you, at the time I was still dealing with other kinds of abuse and low self-esteem. When it came down to being an African American woman, though, I knew that I wouldn't let people talk to me however they wanted to. I was always speaking up for myself and other people.

At another banking organization, I was the first and only Black woman to be on the trading desk.

I just remember always being proud of who I was because I was raised by strong Black women. I'd seen what my mom had gone through being common-law married to a white man. I knew what that dynamic was, seeing people heckle them and experiencing so many very hurtful words because of their relationship. I felt all of that and internalized those very hurtful things. Those were wounds and scars that were emotional, but they hurt just as deeply as physical wounds.

I had to learn very quickly that some people would never like me because of my brown skin. I remember driving through a town in North Carolina with another Black friend. We got stopped by police as we were driving to a Bible conference, and we were wearing our church clothes. The police came up and asked for my license and registration, and my friend kept telling me to "Put your hands on the steering wheel, girl, I want to go home tonight!"

I knew very little about the South at the time, so I thought she was just being overdramatic. Then the cop came back and asked me, "Ma'am, can you read?"

I told him, truthfully, that I didn't even see a speed limit posted. I was so angry that he would ask me that, as if my brown skin somehow made me uneducated. This was around the time when police brutality against the Black community was just beginning to be widely scrutinized and criticized.

He took my information and went back to his car to run my information, then came back to thank me for my service with my church. After he'd just deeply insulted me! It made me wonder if he would have treated a white woman in the same way, and how he might have treated me if I wasn't affiliated with my church.

As a pastor, I experienced a lot of racism from my senior leaders. They never gave me the opportunity to be in the public eye or to spread the gospel message to the masses. He, especially, wanted to keep me in the shadows. I served as a pastor in Alabama, Mississippi, and Louisiana, and in every posting, I experienced racism from leaders within my church. It was almost like there was a target on my back.

Even in those circumstances, God was using that. He needed me to learn who I was, and he needed to show those leaders that they couldn't break me. As Keke Palmer said, "You can't break Black women because we've already been broken open." Imagine everything we have been through, and all we've had to endure.

Enduring being told that our natural hair is unprofessional. Being told that we don't "look the part." Getting flack for choosing to wear our natural looks. Being called "brave" just for existing in our natural state. Our hair represents who we are, and for someone to say that it's a problem for them, there's something wrong.

Those wounds hurt. Those scars affect our self-esteem and identity. As little girls, we're shown straight hair and shiny, curly hair and told that's the standard of beauty. Then we look in the mirror and come to terms with the beautiful 4C coils God has blessed us with. We must go through a process of realizing that our natural hair is just as beautiful as long, blonde hair. We are all unique in his eyes.

Now, people who know me know that I love my wigs. But that isn't because I don't love my natural hair. I was always super confident with my hair, whether it was long as a child, or shorter later. My low self-esteem stemmed from within and was caused by my father's abandonment.

If I had gone through therapy prior to 2015, I may have never gotten involved with a church that ended up abusing me spiritually. That's truly how much it changed my self-worth and helped me heal my wounds. And yet, God still used that. I don't think it was a mistake, I think God allowed it because it was part of the journey, I needed to be on to develop discipline in my spiritual walk.

Prior to becoming a pastor and going through seminary, I didn't know how to sit still with God. I was trying to fake it until I made it, until I got to a point where I didn't want to fake it anymore. I wanted to faith it until I made it. So, even though I did end up leaving my church because of the racism and spiritual abuse I experienced, being a pastor gave me the spiritual discipline my soul had so desired, even though my mind didn't know it.

It allowed me to get to a place of obedience. And that's what God calls us to. He doesn't call us to a thing, to a job, or even to a person. He calls us to follow him and be obedient to his call. A lot of people think that when God calls you to a certain ministry or vocation, you're supposed to stay there forever. But if that were the case, where would obedience come in? You might become complacent in that place, even to the point of disobedience.

There were lots of moments of disobedience in my life. There was even a time where I ran away from God because I was trying to avoid being wounded. I was nineteen years old, and my Bishop laid hands on me and told me that I was called to ministry. I'd grown up in the church, I'd gone every Sunday, and I knew how church folk were. They were hypocrites and liars, and they were dealing with wounds that I never wanted. So, I left the church.

Only to end up becoming a minister decades later, covered in wounds because of my low self-esteem and disobedience to God. It is crazy how many wounds I got from the world. Sometimes our wounds are self-inflicted. Sometimes our wounds are allowed by God to strengthen our faith.

I can admit that a lot of my wounds were self-inflicted. We can blame God for a lot of our scars, but if we really look deep into the wounds, we were the cause.

Do you realize who God called you to be? You are royalty. Take a moment to process that. Your position cannot be denounced because God has crowned you with His love. No mistake or corrupted idea can keep you from God's mercy, grace, and compassion. Nobody is too far from God's saving Grace, regardless of what they have done. He loves you.

Sometimes, to heal your wounds, you're going to have to let God dig deep and pull out some of that pain. Your wounds will never heal if they're infected, and often to get the infection out, you must cause more pain to root it out. You will bleed out on people if you don't allow him to work on your heart and feel all your pain.

And that's how you win wounded. God will prepare you for your best season by allowing you to become wounded in the darkest seasons of your life. He will turn your trauma into testimony. He will turn your pain into purpose. He will turn your mess into His message. He will turn your scars into sacrifice. He will turn your wounds into winning. He will birth those wins out of brokenness. And then he will let you show your wounds to others so that they feel encouraged to share their own wounds and begin healing. Your wounds serve a purpose.

Never forget that Jesus is the ultimate example of winning wounded. He never covered up his scars. He let us see his wounds so that we could see what it cost him to bring us freedom.

Isaiah 53:5

"But he was pierced for our transgressions, he was crushed for our iniquities; the punishment that brought us peace was on him, and by his wounds, we are healed."

CHAPTER 6

Releasing You and Freeing Me

"You cannot love what you choose not to forgive."

The last few chapters have been heavy. And, truthfully, forgiveness can be heavy too. But after everything I've mentioned in the last few chapters, I wanted to approach this chapter from the perspective of lifting burdens. Jesus talks about forgiveness many times throughout Scripture, and I believe that we cannot know God unless we learn how to forgive.

When I think about forgiveness, one Bible story that resonates with me is the story of the sinful woman (Luke 7:36-50), because I felt like I was a sinful woman. This woman heard about Jesus coming to town, and she did everything she could to get to Jesus, even though she knew she was living a sinful life. When she saw Jesus, she collapsed at his feet weeping in tears and began to wash his feet with her hair.

It reminded me of moments in my life when I felt completely defeated and broken in my life and poured all I had onto Jesus. And just like the woman, he told her that her sins had been forgiven. You're whole. And I felt like that in my own journey. For me to be able to forgive other people the way Jesus had forgiven me, I had to understand that I wasn't perfect.

I'm not saying that my abusers, or any of the people in my life who'd caused me pain, were less at fault for what they'd done. However, I had to take a hard look in the mirror and do some evaluation and self-reflection to discover areas in my life that may have caused me to put myself in these situations.

I had low self-worth. I didn't know who I was in Christ. I was a hurt person hurting other people, and that saying is true for all of us. Hurt people do hurt people. I don't care who you are, if you're hurting in some kind of way, you're going to project that hurt onto someone else. When it comes to forgiveness, we need to dig deeply into ourselves and see where in our lives we have unresolved unforgiveness. Even toward our own selves.

I had a lot of unforgiveness for myself because I hung onto hating my dad for so many years because he abandoned me. Because of that, I ended up in abusive relationships that caused me significant damage. I had to unwind some things and really look deep within myself and say, "Sonya, you must forgive yourself. Jesus has forgiven you, why are you still holding onto unforgiveness?"

You cannot love what you choose not to forgive.

So, I really wasn't loving myself. When you choose not to forgive yourself, you don't love yourself. They can't work together. For me, I realized I was the common denominator in the whole journey of forgiveness.

I believe forgiveness liberates you—I felt so liberated when I started to forgive myself. Hey, bad things happened. Yes, I was in one bad relationship after another. Yes, I made bad choices and mistakes, but God has forgiven me. So, it's time for me to live my present story so that my future self can thrive. I really had to work on forgiving Sonya.

Forgiveness is not for someone else; it's for you. When you learn and choose to forgive yourself, you're able to live in the life that God has given you freely. A life full of joy, full of peace, full of hope.

It is a journey. It's layers and layers of peeling back brokenness.

We know you love Jesus, but there was a point in your life when you weren't a lover of Jesus. There was a point in your life when there was a lot of unresolved brokenness and unforgiveness that wasn't allowing you to heal. God had to help you work through it and heal.

That's all I want people to understand. The Sonya that you see today, thanks be to Jesus, God had to do a lot of work on, especially as it relates to unforgiveness. I didn't just arrive. He had to take this broken vessel, just like the woman who washed Jesus' feet, and work good out of it.

A lot of times, the journey looks different for every person. Sometimes it can be years of unwinding unforgiveness—depending on the depths of the brokenness. I think that we have to be honest with where we are.

I'm hurting.

This hurts, God.

Don't act like it doesn't hurt when you're talking to God. Don't pretend that it doesn't hurt you. You aren't helping yourself. He already knows. Tell him, "They hurt me, and I don't know what to do with this pain."

That's the point I came to. I was hurt to the point of wanting to commit suicide, having depression, panic attacks, anxiety. In my life, it was down to a lot of unforgiveness. I'm no therapist, but I can say that for my life, the root was unforgiveness.

Anxiety, depression, and a lot of negative self-talk is rooted in unforgiveness.

Sitting in that pain and allowing God to heal you can help you overcome that pain. You have to feel what you feel. It's a painful process, and sometimes we do everything we can to numb the pain.

I had a friend remind me of this when I left my ministry. I was trying to escape the pain. I thought, "I don't want to feel this, these people hurt me! They were supposed to be Christians!" So, I thought, if no one should ever hurt you, it should not be the church.

But what do you do when it is the church? What do you do when it's your spiritual leader? The people you're supposed to trust the most.

When that happens, you end up broken. That's why a lot of people run from the church. They run to self-medication because they're hurt.

Unaddressed unforgiveness can drive you to very sinful places. It needs to be dealt with and given to Jesus.

That's what I want to help you to understand. It's okay not to be okay. It's okay to sit in your hurt and feel it. But it's not okay to stay there. It's not okay to stay broken. It's not okay to walk in unforgiveness. When we choose to forgive and release our brokenness to God, it springs forth a liberation that says I am human, my burdens may be many, but His strength is made perfect in my weakness.

Scripture tells us that if we want Jesus to forgive us, we must forgive others (The Lord's Prayer). One of the greatest commandments is to love your neighbor as yourself, but how can you love your neighbor if you don't love yourself? How can you love yourself if you won't forgive yourself? To truly walk in agape love, you must forgive yourself.

From a biblical perspective, you cannot love what you choose not to forgive. You want peace that passes all understanding, but you won't gain that unless you forgive yourself. You want a joyful life? Hard to obtain that without forgiving. You want his blessings to rain down on you? You can't obtain that without forgiveness.

We block our own blessings because we are stuck in the pit of unforgiveness. Our blessings are held up because we won't forgive. Other people move on with their lives twenty times over, but we are stuck.

If I had continued to hold my abuser's hostage in my thoughts, I would have missed out on Lee. God would have presented him to me in a nice bow, but I would have missed him because I was still walking in unforgiveness with my abusers. It would have shown up in trust issues. Because unforgiveness creates trust issues and self-sabotage issues.

I wouldn't have been able to see my gift. I would have also treated him the same way I treated all my other situations. And that's why God had to heal me of my unforgiveness because what he had for me was so beautiful, he didn't want me to mess it up. He told me I still had unforgiveness, so I had to forgive my abusers. They weren't bigger than what He had for me.

We hold on to unforgiveness as a crutch. But God says to forget those things and focus on the mark. To press forward toward the mark, the prize that God has for us.

Forgiveness is a confession from your mouth to God's ears to your soul. Part of you needs to understand and recognize the things that you did wrong. When we're honest about our faults, and the part we play in our own pain, we can get that burden lifted off us.

When I went back into ministry with the church that had previously abused me, I knew it was the wrong thing. But so much of my flesh felt like it was a comfortable place, and it was all I knew. God was screaming, "no" at me, but when I made the decision, God allowed me to go back because it was my desire, and He had to demonstrate to me that it was not what He wanted for me. There were a lot of lessons I had to learn in that season, especially how sometimes disobedience can be on a path that looks Godly. God will never make us follow His instructions. He will let us go it alone until we realize that His path is always the best—a lesson that is frequently difficult to learn.

Now, don't get me wrong. Being in ministry wasn't a sin, but going back into a situation I knew God didn't want me in, and being disobedient so that I could be comfortable, was a sin. It was never God's will for me to go back to that place, but he allowed me to do it.

He allows disobedience for a time and for a purpose. He used that situation, but He knew that wasn't the right path for me, just like he knew marrying an abusive man was not the right path for me. Yet he allowed me to do what I thought was right and used those situations to show me things about myself and areas of my life where I needed to be more faithful. It was all purposeful, but it was never what He wanted for me.

There are good things that look enticing and correct to us, but the enemy can pervert them because of our disobedience. Eventually, though, God will call us out of our sinfulness. And when he heals us, we must forgive ourselves.

Many times, we do disobedient things, and we blame God for it. And all he wants us to do is admit that we're wrong. We must take accountability for our disobedience. Instead, we go into hiding, we lie, we change our stories, and it causes even more sin.

We are the common denominator of many of the situations we find ourselves in. Somewhere down the line, we didn't listen to God, and if we really sit down and peel back the layers, we can find where it really started.

What I want you to know is that there's hope for that. There's so much beauty that God can turn from ashes. It happens when we're honest with God and with ourselves. And when we think about forgiveness, it's not about reconciling with another person, it's about reconciliation with God. Your reconciliation with God is the most important thing.

Unforgiveness keeps you separated from God. And he knows that. The journey toward forgiveness is often very hard, but you shouldn't run away from forgiveness, you should run to it. You need it to live the abundant life which God has called us to. (John 10)

The enemy will use unforgiveness repeatedly to kill, steal, and destroy our future. But God came that we might have life, and life abundant. When I surrendered unforgiveness to God, things started looking different in my life. Transformation started to take place. There's so much growth in forgiveness. There's so much spiritual growth that happens when you forgive yourself when you forgive others.

I once had a mentor who loved to talk about forgiveness. He'd seen a lot of things, and a lot of people had done things to him. But what he always did was say, "God bless you," or "Be at peace." I never witnessed him curse the people who threw stones at him, and that was encouraging to me.

It's been encouraging in my life to see leaders be abused and bulldozed and still not have a harsh word to say to their abuser. To still be a blessing to them. When you forgive people, you can bless them and not feel some type of way.

I remember when my abuser found me. I was serving in Biloxi, MS, and I got a call from the front desk that someone had left a message for me. It was my abuser. He'd found me. The receptionist told me that it was urgent, and he wanted me to call him back.

So, I did. I was hesitant to call him back, but I did it. And he said he wanted to know if I would forgive him. What in the world? It had been so many years since our divorce. He said he was sorry for all the pain and the hurt that he had caused and that I didn't deserve the pain that he had caused me. He asked if I would forgive him and if I would pray for him.

I didn't ask him what was going on in his personal life. I was shocked that this man who had physically and mentally abused me, would track me down to say, "I'm sorry for all these things I've done to you. Would you please forgive me? Would you pray for me?"

I think that's what forgiveness does when you surrender it to God. He will take care of your enemies, and sometimes even make them come back to you in humility.

I've never laid eyes on the person who took Rudolph's life. I walked in unforgiveness for years for a person I didn't know. In my mind, I had the right to do so—that person took the life of my daughter's father and my husband. But it caused me a lot of pain because the more I held on to it, the less I could receive from God. My hands were closed in fists, and God needed me to open them.

After that, I had to come to terms with what closure looks like. Finding closure is on you. Stop expecting and waiting for closure from someone that hurt you. Love yourself enough to let go of what was and be open to something new.

I was looking for closure and I was never going to get it. When I meet Jesus, will he reveal it all? It probably won't even matter at that point. I'll just be at the feet of Jesus, not wiping his feet with my wigs. But we'll be having a party!

When we walk in unforgiveness, we walk as victims instead of victors. And we create even more victims because hurt people hurt people. The worst kind of victim is the one who chooses to create another one.

Obviously, my abuser had been a victim at some point in his life, and he chose to make me a victim.

The person who killed Rudolph had been a victim at some point in their life, and they chose to take a man from his family.

It is so hard to see that we're wrong because we're so self-righteous. But there are times when you are wrong! So, get over yourself. Admit that you're wrong. You're not always the victim, and you will not always be the victim.

That same mentor I mentioned earlier once came to me and said, "Stop telling that story about your domestic violence survival. That's not your story anymore. Find a new story. Stop being a victim."

Ooh, that stung.

But he was so right. I wanted to take that show on the road. I was going to run with it forever.

He said, "What is God doing for you now?"

You know why I kept running with that story? Because I hadn't forgiven myself. I wanted to cling to what was familiar, and unforgiveness was very familiar to me. I could deny forgiveness to anyone, especially myself, and still feel "good" about myself. But, of course, I wasn't really feeling good.

I was just wearing a mask. So many people do it—men and women. So many of us live that life as Christians. They're in bad marriages, in bad friendships, in bad relationships. We just must stop and get to a place where we say, "I'm wrong. I'm going to take accountability for my actions."

That's what I did. I realized that God did not want me to marry that man who ended up abusing me. I chose to marry him after all the stop signs, red flags, and yield signs. I did that. When we settle for less than what God has for us, we receive less than what God desires for us.

Whatever it is we're dealing with in our lives, we must take responsibility for our own actions. It's easy for us to blame somebody else for our faults. But if forgiveness is about you, then you need to take accountability for you.

My abusers don't have to stand before God for my sins. I have to stand before God for my sins. When we're walking around with unforgiveness for someone, we are in sin. It is a sin. I don't care how much you go to church if you're preaching, pastoring, whoever you are. If you have unforgiveness in your heart toward yourself or anyone else, you are in sin.

It starts with forgiving yourself and forgiving others, just as God has already forgiven. I'm not saying it's an easy process, but you have to keep surrendering until that burden is lifted. Until you can pray for the person, until you can think of them, and it no longer hurts.

I knew I'd forgive my ex-husband when I could pray for him. When he called me and asked for my forgiveness, I didn't hang up the phone.

I thank God, only God can give you that forgiveness. We cannot forgive on our own.

When a mother loses her child to a drunk driver, that's a painful hurt. But she must forgive the driver.

God can help us through those difficult moments. He did it for me and he can do it for you.

Hurt people hurt people.

Forgiven people forgive people.

CHAPTER 7

Ordinary Just Won't Do

"Love is the essence of who we were meant to be,
share, experience, and value others."

God willing, a couple months after my book is released, I will be fifty-five years old.

It took me a long time to get to the place I'm in now. For years, I struggled with finding peace. For years I struggled with accepting God's agape love for me. Even as a follower of Christ, I questioned how God could love someone like me.

I know I am not alone when I say this. Sometimes it's hard to love ourselves when all we see is our flaws and imperfections, but there is so much beauty in what we think is imperfect.

I questioned myself often, how could I love the Lord with all my heart but not love myself? I was lacking the Lord's peace in my life. I would have peaceful moments but not the peace of God that surpasses all understanding. This caused me to be unstable in my walk with God. But God never gave up on me. His love pursued me and took me back to the loss of my grandmother. The one that loved me more than I ever knew I could be loved until Jesus.

When my beloved grandmother died, I was twelve years old, and my life began to change dramatically. I can remember praying more to

Jesus and talking to him all the time. I would cry myself to sleep because I missed her so much. I didn't understand why God had to take her from me. She loved me so much and I loved her so much.

My grandmother, Mary Magdalene, was a beautiful soul who loved everybody and would give her last to anyone. She taught me how to make biscuits and crochet, and to this day, my homemade biscuits will melt in your mouth. She wasn't much of a churchgoer but she knew the Lord.

Grandma loved unconditionally. She took strangers into her house. Even though she wasn't a churchgoer, she was showing the love of God to strangers. Really, that was when I began to get my first glimpse of unconditional love.

Even though I couldn't really identify what it was, I got to see it and experience it with her. When she died, I really felt a sense of deep grief. Sorrow. Because my grandma was everything to me. She was my best friend and was there for everything I felt I was experiencing and going through as a young girl. I felt like just being around my grandmother, she knew what was going on in my life. I didn't necessarily have to tell her what was wrong to feel better. Just her presence made me feel better.

I think that, a lot of times, that's what love does. That unconditional love does so much for us.

She died of lung cancer when I was twelve. After I lost her, after she he went home to be with Jesus, I started to have this connection with God in a very organic way. I was only twelve, I didn't have the language of prayer yet, even though I grew up in church. I just started trying this thing, you know, talking with God and just randomly praying. Just trying to get closeness with God without really knowing that's what I was doing.

I remember in church, people would always turn and go, "You know God is love and He wants us to love like him."

And I was like, "Okay God! Give me a heart like yours."

And I didn't really know what that meant. I was praying, God, give me a heart like yours, not knowing that God's heart is huge and has the capacity to be loved and be broken. So, during that period, that's where all that came from. I wanted a heart like God, I desired a heart that could love like God. I wanted to deeply love the way my grandmother loved. I saw God in the way she connected with people.

Have you ever heard that phrase, "You may be the first representative of Jesus people, see?"

That's what I saw in my grandmother, even though she wasn't a churchgoer. She made me want to get to know God. Her death brought me closer to God.

My compassion for young people stems from the brokenness I experienced, so when I witness young people going through terrible times, I often think back to where I came from, the people who heard me, and the people who helped me. With that, I have committed my life to serving young people and teaching them to love God and to know their identity is in Him.

On Thursday, August 1, 2019, the Lord called home three precious angels to be with Him in eternity, Travis Roberson, Eric Smith, and Javonte (Tae) Johnson. These young men served and attended my church. I was their Pastor, friend, and leader. They were like sons to me. Tae had joined the church that past April, and Travis and Eric were going to finish their classes at the end of the month. They were vibrant, funny, and loved life. They loved their families and friends, and our church was like a second home to them.

They pursued the Lord with all their heart. I was deeply saddened, and my heart was shattered by their death. Even as a Pastor, I just couldn't understand why the Lord would take three beautiful souls at the age of fourteen. However, I took joy in knowing that these young men accepted Jesus in their hearts, and they desired to live for Him. Travis, Tae, and Eric touched the lives of many people including mine and they are so deeply missed. They were loved by all and most of all by God.

They are with our Heavenly Father, sitting at the feet of Jesus and there is no better place to be. I can hear them saying to me now, "Why are you crying Pastor., we are ok, you told us about Jesus, and we are with

Him. It is ok." Thank you, Lord, for these three beautiful gifts that you allowed to be in this world for such a short time that has made such an impact. Knowing them personally has made me better than I was before I met them. They taught me that young people just need to know that the Lord has not forgotten about them, and He desires a relationship with them because He loves them. No one is too far from God's reach and these young men knew Jesus and they were destined for greatness. Their passing will not be in vain, God will be gloried in this tragedy. Their passing will lead many souls to Jesus and lives will be transformed for God's glory.

The most beautiful relationship you will ever experience is one with Jesus. Falling in love with Jesus is the best thing you will ever do!

Ordinary Just Won't Do by Commissioned, is one of my favorite gospel songs of all time. It brought me through some difficult times.

When we look around our world today, it is so evident that people are hurting and lacking the love of Jesus.

How we see the love of God in one another.

They died loving one another. One saw the other drown and tried to save him. Then the last one tried to save the other two. All three of them died trying to save one another. It was like Scripture coming off the paper. We got to witness that in real life. We got to see it in real time.

But it was super painful. I had all their mothers looking to me to minister to them. Those boys were part of my congregation. When they were gone, I remember their moms coming to me and asking to do the eulogy for each one. I didn't know how I could do that; I was broken.

I remember calling my mom and her telling me that I had to do it. They were my young people. And all the young people that loved them would need answers. Who else would give them answers? I was their pastor.

Another mentor of mine told me I needed to get ahead of the grief. He told me everyone would come to me for answers. And I remember praying to God and he gave me this Scripture:

"Greater love has no one than this: to lay down one's life for one's friends." John 15:13

That's the Scripture that I preached at their funerals. That's what they did. That was no ordinary love that they had for each other.

We look for these ordinary types of love. And they may satisfy. They may fill a void here or there. But you will never be whole until you've experienced the love of Jesus Christ. That unconditional love that sees your soul. All your soul. Everything that's laid inside of your soul— the darkness too.

That's the kind of love that I believe we are all longing for and chase after. In things, in drugs, in women, in men, in food, and clothing, in counterfeits. And when I saw this happen, I felt like it was a gift God had given us.

I was working on the eulogies. The moms wanted their children to have individual services. I had to do three eulogies within twenty-four hours. I had to go deep into the love of God. God helped me, because who was I to be standing in front of the congregation and delivering this message? There were so many other people who could have done it, but their mothers asked me specifically.

Because I loved those boys. I loved them. I ministered Christ to them, and they knew that their sons were saved because of the way I loved them. That's exactly what each of them said to me when they asked me to do the eulogies.

I remember the last conversation I had with each of the boys. I remember speaking with Tae a week before it happened. He was crying and I asked him what was wrong. He wanted to know if God really forgave him because he'd done some really bad things in his life. I told him he was fourteen, with his whole life ahead of him, and yes, God had forgiven. He had prayed the prayer of forgiveness and God had forgiven him.

He wanted his brother to know Jesus and know the love that he was already experiencing. I hugged him and he was so excited, he was about to join the football team. And I remember getting the call.

I remember Eric in Sunday school, just goofing off like he normally did. He wanted to know if God would forgive him for smoking weed. In the Sunday School class. And all the kids started to laugh, and I told them,

"This is serious, don't laugh!" He wanted to be saved right there, so I asked the kids to stretch their hands out. And Eric, in that moment, prayed for forgiveness and gave his life to Christ.

Travis, I remember a week before, was asking for the big Bible on the holiness table. I remember my senior pastor complaining, "He can't touch that, Bible. He can't have that, Bible!" I looked at him and said, "It's a Bible!" I told his mother where she could find it and buy it, but she never did get around to buying it before he passed. I gave her that Bible at the service.

All three boys always sat next to me at church. They loved me; they were like my children. Although they were rough around the edges, a lot of people didn't want to be bothered with them, I knew what it was like when people tried to throw me away. I wanted them to know the same kind of love that God had for me. So, after they passed, I had three chairs dedicated in their name, and I left them sitting next to me in the front row.

That's the kind of love God wants us to have. They didn't need an ordinary kind of love. They wanted the type of love that, even if they messed up, by saving each other, they didn't hesitate. That's the kind of love we're supposed to have for another.

Am I willing to lay down my life for my sister or my brother? Absolutely! But do we see that kind of love portrayed often? No, we don't. We see selfishness. We see, "Gimme, gimme." We don't see that type of love in the body of Christ. It is very far and few between. Because if you don't have something to give me, then I'm not going to do it for you. If you hurt me, then I'm not going to love you.

But the Bible clearly talks about loving your enemies, blessing those who curse you. How many times are you supposed to forgive? Seventy times seven? Love! Love your enemies! A lot of times we say that we love God vertically, but God tells us that we can't love him if we don't love our brothers and sisters.

Don't tell me that you love God, and you don't love your brother that you see every day. You walk by the man on the street that's hungry, and you love God. Stop. Absolutely not! We need to talk about the kind of love that we are supposed to have for one another. The kind of love that you cannot possess without the Holy Spirit.

Love wins. Love conquers. Love covers a multitude of sins. You want to win somebody to Christ? Just try loving them. Try meeting them where they are without judgment. Just like I loved those boys.

Even as painful as that experience was, I was so blessed. I was so blessed by a deeper love that I found in God. That God would allow me to witness such a thing that changed, not just my life, but the lives of their families, and all the people in the community. No one could believe that three teenage boys would risk their lives to save each other.

We need to understand that the love we have for one another really comes from the love that we're supposed to have for God. The kind of love that God has for us. Everything else aside.

Sure, you're supposed to love your children, but what about somebody else's child? What about that person in your life who just gets on your last nerve, but who keeps showing up every day? There's a reason why that person is always there. There's an exchange that's supposed to happen. You're supposed to give that person love, and in exchange, you're going to learn how to love and humility.

A lot of times we don't want to go that deep because we're not loving. And we really aren't walking in love or loving ourselves. Any time someone comes to me seeking counsel about a relationship with a loved one, I ask them, "What does your love walk look like? How's the tank? Are you empty? Half full? You need to go to the gas station and get a top up."

What does your love tank look like? Don't look for someone else to love you before you show them love. That's not how this works. Because when you die and meet Jesus, he's going to ask us, "How did you love me? How did you love my people?"

It may be easy for us to put a few dollars in the offering bucket, but how are we really showing love? This is where it comes in. When we experience that kind of love for God, you are living your most authentic self.

People ask me all the time why I'm so joyful, especially despite the things that I've been through. It's because joy consumes me. I'm living in the overflow. You're getting the overflow. I'm full. You're seeing the overflow of God's love spilling out of me. If I wasn't full, it would be hard for me to give it away. And love isn't love unless you give it away. So, what people see in me is literally the overflow.

You want to be so full of love that people are getting it and it's not hard to give. It's hard to give it because you can't give somebody what you don't have. If I have 20 percent, I'm going to try to hold onto it because I need it for myself. But when you're full enough, you have enough to pour out.

That's why Jesus had enough to pour out. Because he *is* love. We are created in his image, so we are meant to be love. You should be able to walk in love and pour it out with no problems. How I'm able to do that is because I've been hurt so much. It's given me the full experience. And I'm just thankful.

True love is agape love. I wish people would walk around asking, "Do you agape me?" Do you agape your enemies? Because that's unconditional, that's the way God loves.

When I went through the experience of losing those boys, I had the chance to see firsthand, in real time, what it meant to love. I'm not saying I want to experience that kind of thing every day, but that deep pain allowed me to experience and appreciate deep love.

What God really wants is for us to know how much he loves us. He sent his son to die for us. Jesus left heaven to die for us. That's no ordinary type of love. What kind of king bleeds for his soldiers? What kind of God dies for his children? Only one who truly loves. Who is LOVE!

When I was twelve, this was the prayer I prayed. If you want to love the way Jesus does, if you're ready to experience no ordinary love, you can pray this prayer too.

"Jesus, I want to have a heart like yours, please give me a heart like yours, Jesus. Please make me more like you," was my constant prayer request to the Lord.

Let the beauty of love be witnessed to all.

Help me to love people for who they are and not for what I want them to be.

Make it my mission and determination to love everybody.

Amen.

CHAPTER 8

God is Changing Your Story

"You will never change from what does not challenge you."

There was a woman I once knew who was very active in church. She served in various leadership roles. She led multiple Bible studies, women's Sunday school, teen programs, and participated in volunteering. She served God and His people selflessly. One morning, she was confronted by her Pastor. The Pastor said to the woman, "Your walk is not authentic, you come to church ministering to these women, and you go home living another life." The woman looked at her Pastor with shame and guilt, and she began to cry. The woman asked her Pastor, "How did you know?" And her Pastor said, "Because I was once you." The woman had been living a double life that she tried desperately to hide. The woman was saved, but she lived in bondage. She was ministering the Good News of Jesus Christ, His Salvation, and Redemption that can change and transform lives, but she did not believe it for her own life. She was being physically, mentally, and emotionally abused in her private life. But God . . . The Lord used this woman's Pastor to speak life into this woman's dead situation. She didn't know that she had a seat at God's table because she didn't believe God could ever love and accept her with all her flaws.

I was once that woman—broken, rejected, abandoned, and thrown away. But thanks to God's redemptive grace, I get to sit with Jesus in the greatest seat in the house. Even at my lowest points, He never gave up on me. I wouldn't be here right now if not for the blood of Jesus. I am a conqueror. I have a Savior who is not just with me, but He lives inside of me. No matter where we go, God is there waiting patiently for us. His presence is always in the room!

God is Changing Your Story and God's picture of your true self is all that matters. As children, we may have been infatuated with royalty but not many of us are conscious of how powerful we really are. We go through life seeking validation from all other sources but God. It becomes a detrimental cycle to our spiritual and mental well-being. We say we don't want to be alone, so we find ourselves looking for love in all the wrong places. We go from heartbreak to heartbreak, blaming ourselves when the issue has never been us. It has always been the distorted image of ourselves that we see in the mirror.

My question for you right now is what you see when you look in the mirror. Do you see a Proverbs 31:25 woman? "She is clothed with strength and dignity; she can laugh at the days to come."

As I think about what it means for "God is changing your story," I'm reminded that God has given us all a story. We all have an opportunity to tell the story that He has given us through our lives. Sometimes those stories are very hard, sometimes they're joyful, sometimes you know you want to forget about it. And I think that when we come to those crossroads in our lives, we must always reflect to where God was in areas where we didn't necessarily see Him. We have to look at those moments and say, well, if God did that then, then He can do that now.

Changing your story means a lot for me because there are so many facets of my life where I've seen God, and how he changed the trajectory when the enemy was trying to snuff my life out. God intervened when the enemy was trying to make me lose my mind. God regulated my mind. When the enemy tried to make me feel like I wasn't worthy of God's love, God came in and consumed me with his love. That changed my story.

Because it's really His story; I just get to tell the story that he has created in me. I think that when we look at it from that perspective, we just get to be participants of what God is doing in us. He just needs a body, a willing vessel. So, when I got to that place in my life to really understand that what I'm going through in my life is all for the glory of God, I started to really understand that my life is just not my own. My life belongs to God, and He's just changing my story.

He changed the story of Mary Magdalene. She was a woman who was possessed with seven demonic spirits. The Bible doesn't specify what these spirits were, but they plagued her and enslaved her. I think about the spirits that I've carried in my own life. Some depression, some anxiety, all these things that the enemy tried to place on me. God had to deliver me from those things.

God changed her story. She became a follower of Jesus Christ. She became one of the first apostles to tell of Jesus' resurrection. And when we look at our lives, we can't just say this is where I am, and this is where I'm going to stay. God wants to change our story. The point of it all is that you get to choose if you want to be a participant in what God is doing in your life. There's this work that must be done for you. There has to be a process of peeling back the layers of a lot of things that we have taken on in our lives. And God is saying that's not what I have for you, daughter. That's not what I have for you, son.

Young people especially, who don't know who they are, tend to dabble in a lot of different things. This world has told them, "If you have stuff, you'll have everything you need. Just collect more, fill your body with more, define your worth by what you have." They're not taught the right things of God, and what they're learning is to be a copycat. And God doesn't call us to be a copycat.

He's calling us to be who he's called us to be. I think it's so important for young people to understand that. You may have been brought up in that household with a single parent like me, and you may have been told that you're never going to be anything. You may have been told that you're never going to amount to anything because your daddy was no good. People tell you, "Your daddy slept around while your mama was on drugs, and you're never going to be anything."

You don't have to accept those lies. Instead, you can accept what God has said about you. He says that you are somebody because of Him. I think whatever you want in your life, if you don't like it, God can change things for good for you. Wherever you are in your life, you don't have to stay there.

For example, my mom was young when she had me. She had an eighth-grade education, and she came to a place where she didn't want it to be her story anymore. So, she went back and got her GED. Who helped to change that story? God did it! She was in her late thirties or early forties when she went back to do that, because she had been raising her children for so long. And it wasn't too late for her to change her story. It's not too late for you now.

So many people make up so many excuses for why they can't live this transformational life, this abundant life God has called us to. So many times, you simply decide that you can't, so you don't try for the better. It must come from within. You just have to believe that, with God, all things are possible.

A lot of times, not always, but a lot of times, you're in the plot line you're in because of decisions that you made. Yet God can redeem, and he can turn everything around, no matter where you are. He has that power. But you must be prepared to live a different story. You can't take the old you into a new season. You have to allow God to not just change your story, but also change your character.

With changing your character, changing your mindset, getting rid of that stinking thinking, God can change you. He can change the way you think about yourself. You simply have to ask God to help you. That transformation has to take place as God is trying to change your story and those are the things that God wants to work on to develop your character.

I remember when I started this journey, really walking with God. People kept reminding me of the old Sonya. Because that's what the enemy wants to do. You're moving forward and you're excited, you can see that you're a different person. You can look in the mirror and see yourself and think, "I'm not the same person anymore." It's nothing to do with looks; it's about the way you feel about yourself and your confidence.

People that know you the way you were will always try to remind you of what you used to do, who you used to be. And that's the devil. That's not to say that they are the devil, but the enemy is using their words to tear you down. Because what does he do? He comes to kill, steal, and destroy.

Also, often, people are more comfortable with the way you used to be. Even as God is changing your story, you may have to change your friends. There will be people that you used to hang out with, but you don't do those things anymore. I don't sit around and talk about people anymore. I don't drink. I don't do those things anymore. So as God is changing your story, your surroundings also change. Your community may now have to change because it must line up with the new creation that God is working in.

You can't put new wine in old wineskin, and you can't put new friends into the old person that you were. And you may not be able to bring your old friends into the new life that God is developing you into. He wants you to surround yourself with like-minded people, people that are on the same journey of wanting to be more like Jesus. Not that we're trying to be perfect. Only Christ is perfect. But if we want God to change us, we must make sure that we're surrounding ourselves with people that are on the same path.

So many people will always try to remind you of who you were because they don't see your growth. They'll say, "What do you think you are doing? Who do you think you are? You can't do that; you're not worthy of that story." Like they said about Jesus, can anything good come out of Nazareth? Can anything good come out of Brooklyn, NY? That's why you can't tell everybody what you're doing. Listen, you better not tell everybody what you are doing in your life all the time. Social media is terrible for that, because people will put everything that they're doing on social media.

And I know that you're excited about what you're doing. I know you want to share it with the whole world but use discernment. God will tell you when to share it and whom to share it with. God is changing your story, and it's not for everybody to know. Everybody's not going to know when God is going to do certain things in your life. Some things God is doing are just for you and Him to know about. There are some things that

God is doing in your life that you can share with a small group of people. Then for some things, he's going to say, "OK. Tell the masses." That's where discernment takes place.

You have to ask God, "Is this just for me and you, or is this for me and my small community? Or is this for me and everybody else?" Because everybody is not cheering you on. They're not! And it's better that they don't know anything, because they're not doing anything with their lives, and they'll look at you with jealousy. Even as I was writing this book, hardly anybody knew. There was just a small group of people that were aware, because people might have tried to discourage me, to tell me that I would fail, that I didn't have a story to tell.

However, when God changes your story, you become a completely new person. There are areas of your life that God wants to focus on, and it is no one's business. You must be in your secret place, in your closet with God. Because when people see the new you, they're going to hit that rewind button. They're going to try and compare you to who you are, to the person that He changed.

"Who do you think you are. Girl, you aren't better than us. You were just in the club with us a few months ago." They're going to remind you of all your old sins, because they don't want you to get better.

Consider this too, though. Not only can you not carry your old friends and your old lifestyle into your new life, but unless you shed your old life, you can't fit the new people and the new blessings and the new opportunities. If you really want God to transform you, if you really want Him to rewrite your story, you must be both feet in. You must be committed. You might think, "Well, I'm going to church and I'm doing things a little better. But I'm also still smoking weed on the weekends and still have one foot in my old lifestyle."

However, your new blessings do not exist in your previous lifestyle, nor do they exist for the old you. They are not for that person. They are for the new transformed person. And know that it's going to take a process. It's not a sprint, but a marathon. And as God continues to change you,

you must keep in mind that you have to be able to accept where you are in the process.

Yes, it may be a struggle. Yes, it may be hard. And everybody's struggle looks different in their life. Everybody. It doesn't matter if you're dealing with cancer or another type of illness, losing a job, marital difficulties, or simply having a bad day. We all struggle. So, we must remember that as God is changing our story, He may be changing our sisters' and brothers' stories, and we don't have to compete with them. I don't have to complete because I know that while God is working on you, He's working on me as well. God can work on fifty people at the same time, fifty million people even, at the same time!

A lot of the time, we want to resist and give God some pushback because it feels uncomfortable. I don't like how this feels, God. How come my journey is difficult right now and someone else's isn't? Well, that's not your journey. God wants you to be present and be accepting of the journey He has you on, not looking left or right and worrying what someone else's journey looks like. After all, you have no idea what struggles they're facing in their secret place.

Even after Mary's first encounter with Jesus, she becomes someone that He knew could be trusted to share his resurrection with others. Even though the brothers didn't believe her, He revealed it to her first. Jesus became the center of her whole entire world. And that's what we must remember. Even as God is working on us and it can be very, very uncomfortable in our lives, we have to accept it and acknowledge that this is going to be good for us because God knows best.

We must embrace whom God has called us to be. Psalm 139:12 says, "For You created my inmost being. You knit me together in my mother's womb. I praise you because I am fearfully and wonderfully made. Your works are wonderful, I know that full well." Didn't you know? That God created you beautifully and wonderfully. Believe that what God has for you is best. And what God has for you is for you. I don't have to want what my brother or sister has. I want what God has for me because it's specific for me. He handpicked this thing for me, and only I can operate in that gift because it's unique for me.

A lot of times, we can look at our brothers and sisters and want what they have. And then we get that, and it doesn't look the same way for us. It doesn't work the same way because it was never intended for us to have and to work in. It's just like when David told Saul, "I'm not fighting in your gear. I must use my own stuff. This little slingshot and pebble may look little like nothing to you, but God gave me this to use. So, I'm going to slay this giant with it."

God is changing our story. We've got to think about the things that God is doing in us and how He is going to use us with the gifts and abilities that He has given to us. Not what we want Him to give us. Not what somebody else has. I want what God is giving me. Imagine that your life is a puzzle, and the gifts God has given you are pieces. When you desire gifts that are for someone else, they are not going to fit into your life because they were not meant to fit. What is for someone else you know is not for you.

We must ask for discernment to discover if we want something because it's a desire from God, or because we're jealous of what someone else has. We have to check our motives and discover what's behind our desires. Do I really want this because I want God to be glorified in it? Or is it because I'm jealous?

What is jealousy really rooted in? It's a lack of self-worth. It's the feeling that you feel less than somebody. Jealousy has caused people to kill. That's what happened with Cain and Abel. That was Satan's whole thing, too. That's why he got kicked out. His pride, his jealousy, and wickedness. So, we've got to be mindful of all those things.

I think the beauty of God changing our story is that the creator of heaven and earth is taking the time not only just to create, but to give us this amazing, beautiful story of who He is through us. It's His story; we just get to narrate it. We get to narrate the great author's story, which was what I wanted to do in this book. I get to narrate God's story of my life to other people, and maybe through it, they would come to know Jesus as Lord and Savior and one day get to narrate His story through them.

It's His story. The whole Bible. When people read the Bible, they shouldn't be reading it as if it's about them. The Bible is about God. Yes, we absolutely benefit from what the Bible says, but we can't forget that it's about Him. So, if we are reading the Bible and we think it's about us, that goes back to motives. I used to read the Bible thinking, "Well, that was really nice of you, God, to throw that in for me three thousand years ago. That was so thoughtful." But the Bible isn't my story. It's God's story from creation to a few years after the resurrection. The story He is writing for me is unique to me.

We are living in end times. God wants to change our story. He wants people to come to know Him. And you can't come to know Jesus without Him changing your story. That's really what this is. He wants to change our story. And not only is He changing our story, but He is changing the entire narrative of who false prophets say He is. We must get to this place where we're using this voice that God gave us. Because they're telling these lies and they're saying He doesn't speak anymore, and He doesn't perform miracles anymore. He's not listening, and he's abandoned us.

But look at your life! God changed what happened to you. He turned your test into a testimony. You can't tell me He's not working because I've seen the evidence. That's exactly why sharing our stories is so powerful. God is still doing miracles! God is still opening the blind eyes and bringing the dead to life and healing the sick. He is still doing, still changing people's stories.

Every time I hear about somebody being healed from something; God changed their story. Every time I hear about somebody surviving cancer, God changed their story. Every time I hear about God doing something in someone's life that they didn't expect, God has changed their story.

Who does that? Who? Who's doing that? I can't take credit for that. A doctor can't take credit for that. God is the one that's changing the story. And we get to tell the narrative and tell it truthfully. And don't take any credit. If God has changed your story, you give God the glory. You don't take credit for that. Say who did it! Say it proud and loud. That is how people come to know God.

The ones that are on the fence, the ones that feel like God has left them, the ones who feel rejected. The ones that think that God doesn't answer at all. There are so many people that think God doesn't answer prayer. But when you profess about what God has done in your life, it's beautiful. God can use your story to change the trajectory of someone else's.

If He didn't want to change our story, He wouldn't have sent Jesus!

We were all destined for Hell! But God changed our story by sending His only Son (John 3:16). Why? That in itself. You don't need anything else! He already changed our story when He sent his son, Jesus. The devil at one point, he tried his best to tear down God's Kingdom and God said, "not so."

Start reading the New Testament, and you see what happened. We begin to see in those chapters what happened. The story unfolds and you begin to see God changing the story.

Some people's stories would have never been changed if Jesus didn't come. It was the ultimate rewrite. With ultimate plot twists. Without Him, we would be burning. And that's real talk. We couldn't save ourselves. We were destined for hell.

How many times did the Israelites get themselves in trouble after God delivered them? He kept working with them in mercy and grace. And finally, He had to send His son, Jesus, because those goats were not listening. God knew that if He wanted it done right, He had to do it Himself. So, He did. And it was the ultimate game changer.

I am so thankful for that. I'm just so thankful He gave me a story. And I used to say, this may not have been the story I wanted to live. But, yes, I would have. Because I know now who I am and who I belong to.

I want to remind you to stay on the course. Your story is already written. That's the beautiful part. God is changing your story, but how can He change a story that's already written? Well, because He knows the ending. He knows where you're supposed to end up. And sometimes you might make decisions that get you off your plotline, but there is no plotline you can go down that God cannot write you out of. He knows the ultimate plan for your life. So, you might be going to a place one way that is not what He wanted for you, and He can turn it around and make it a better story.

He is God and he can take it all together and make something beautiful. Some ashes, maybe, but a lot of beauty, too. You simply have to ask him to come into your life and take the pen out of your hand. You were never meant to write your story. You are not the author, He is. So let Him do what He does best and change your story.

As I end this book, I don't want to miss the opportunity to witness those out there who may be encountering God for the first time. There are so many people who've been walking in darkness for their whole lives, not knowing that there was a better way. Friend, there is a better way. There is The Way, and He wants to turn your life around, to rewrite your story into something more beautiful. If you want Jesus to come into your heart and change your story, pray the prayer below.

Prayer of Salvation

Romans 10:9-10 - Prayer of Repentance

If you declare with your mouth, "Jesus is Lord," and believe in your heart that God raised him from the dead, you will be saved. For it is with your heart that you believe and are justified, and it is with your mouth that you profess your faith and are saved.

Dear God,

In complete sincerity, I come to You with a humble heart and ask You for forgiveness. You know what I've done, You know who've I've been, but today, Lord, I want You to change my story. I want You to come and dwell in my heart and help me to become a new creation. Help me to become more like You.

Father, I want to be Yours, and I want to be the narrator of the story You have for me. Help me put down the pen. Help me to walk by faith and not by sight. Come into my life right now and change who I was so that I can become who You want me to be.

Amen.

SOMETHING TO CONSIDER.

1. In this present moment, how is God rewriting your story?

2. How does your identity in Christ encourage you to keep running your race?

3. How has God's love transformed your life?

4. What are five things that you would tell your younger self?

5. Do you find it hard to forgive those who have hurt or disappointed you?

6. God can restore what's been lost and broken. What do you believe God will restore in your life?

7. Is your faith strong enough to face the big trials of this life? If not, what things could you do to strengthen your faith?

8. How do you trust God in hopeless situations?

UNCHANGING TRUTHS FROM GOD'S WORD

1. God is trustworthy.
   "Trust in the LORD with all your heart and lean not on your own understanding; in all your ways submit to him, and he will make your paths straight." - Proverbs 3:5-6

2. God is for the sinner.
   "I have not come to call the righteous, but sinners." - Mark 2:17

3. God's grace is greater.
   "For it is by grace you have been saved, through faith—and this is not from yourselves, it is the gift of God" - Ephesians 2:8

4. God reveals his glory through his people.
   "You are the light of the world. A town built on a hill cannot be hidden." - Matthew 5:14

5. God works through our weaknesses.
   "My grace is sufficient for you, for my power is made perfect in weakness.' Therefore, I will boast all the more gladly about my weaknesses, so that Christ's power may rest on me." - 2 Corinthians 12:9

6. God is all-sufficient.
   "His divine power has given us everything we need for a godly life through our knowledge of him who called us by his own glory and goodness." - 2 Peter 1:3

7. God gives hope in all circumstances.
   "Fixing our eyes on Jesus, the pioneer and perfecter of faith. For the joy set before him he endured the cross, scorning its shame, and sat down at the right hand of the throne of God." - Hebrews 12:2

8. God is in control and good.
   "I will exalt you, my God the King ... Great is the LORD and most worthy of praise; his greatness no one can fathom ... The LORD is good to all." - Psalm 145:1, 3, 9
   "In His hand is the life of every living thing and the breath of all mankind." Job 12:10

9. God's timing is perfect.
   "There is an appointed time for everything. And there is a time for every matter under heaven." Ecclesiastes 3:1

10. God keeps His promises.
    "God keeps every promise he makes. He is like a shield for all who seek his protection. If you claim that he said something that he never said, he will reprimand you and show that you are a liar." Proverbs 30:5-6

11. God will turn suffering for your good and His Glory, if you allow Him to
    "To give them a beautiful headdress instead of ashes, the oil of gladness instead of mourning, the garment of praise instead of a faint spirit." Isaiah 61:3
    "And we know that for those who love God all things work together for good, for those who are called according to his purpose. "Romans 8:28
    "But they who wait for the Lord shall renew their strength; they

shall mount up with wings like eagles; they shall run and not be weary; they shall walk and not faint." Isaiah 40:31

12. God alone saves us.

"And you also were included in Christ when you heard the message of truth, the gospel of your salvation. When you believed, you were marked in him with a seal, the promised Holy Spirit, who is a deposit guaranteeing our inheritance until the redemption of those who are God's possession—to the praise of his glory." - Ephesians 1:13-14

ABOUT THE AUTHOR

The true funnel toward effective leadership is service. Embodying that preface with the highest of honor is servant leader Sonya D. Wright.

Sonya serves alongside her husband Pastor Lee A. Wright as the Co-Pastor of Elevation Worship Ministries International. She also serves as a second-grade schoolteacher and is an International Best-selling Author. Her altruism establishes her as one known for placing the causes of others above her own. With both social disparity and various forms of injustice towards humanity as her leading passions, she is often a featured speaker on diverse platforms for her devout advocacy.

Sonya's life lessons and experiences have taught her to live life to the fullest and treasure every moment as a gift from God. She has a heart for God and His people. Her past afflictions, trials, and tribulations have been the catalyst that has encouraged her to lead by example, courageously and unapologetically authentic.

Sonya is passionate about her calling to win souls for Christ and love inclusively. Saved to serve is her heart. Kingdom building is her focus. Helping others find their God-given purpose in life is her passion. Trusting the Lord with all her heart is her foundation.

Sonya's motto is clear: *when we tolerate injustice on any level, we are choosing to be comfortable and complex, at the expense of innocent lives, who are suffering at the hands of the oppressor.*

Invoked sincerely by sheer faith in God and the well-being of man-kind, Sonya submits that love is her primary inspiration. She believes love is both a repellent against hatred and the only force credible in bringing transformation to the world.